Employee Management Standards

The L.J. Minor Foodservice Standards Series

VOLUME  4

Employee Management Standards

ROBERT W. McINTOSH

*School of Hotel, Restaurant
and Institutional Management
Michigan State University
East Lansing, Michigan*

AVI PUBLISHING COMPANY, INC.
Westport, Connecticut

Copyright © 1984 by
THE AVI PUBLISHING COMPANY, INC.
Westport, Connecticut

*Cover photograph by Robert W. McIntosh with the cooper-
ation of Gregory Van Drie, General Manager, Carriage Inn
Motel, Manistee, MI.*

*Frontispiece photograph by Stephanie B. Churley with the
cooperation of Ort Pengue, Manager, Polo's Restaurant,
Westport, CT.*

Library of Congress Cataloging in Publication Data

McIntosh, Robert Woodrow, 1917–
    Employee management standards.

    (The L.J. Minor foodservice standards series; v. 4)
    Bibliography: p.
    Includes index.
    1. Personnel management. I. Title. II. Series.
HF5549.M3396 1984   658.3   84-2875
ISBN 0-87055-459-X

ABCDE 3210987654

Printed in the United States of America

The Human Equation

Any action I could take, which might rebound to the benefit of our company, or to any member of the Delta family, I took it . . . immediately, or as soon as possible.

Any word I could speak or write, to express appreciation for a kindness or consideration shown me, or provide useful instruction, or give constructive but gentle criticism, or help redress a wrong; or any word I could speak or write to inspire a person of talent upward and onward, or encourage one who was discouraged, or recognize one worthy of it, or help someone identify and celebrate his/her uniqueness and goodness, I spoke or wrote it . . . immediately, or as soon as possible.

Not surprisingly, in a career affording an infinite variety of such experiences, I have come to the realization that my primary interests have always clustered around the mystery, wonder, and beauty of the human equation.

Charles P. Knecht
(1911–1980)
Vice President Delta Airlines

Contents

Preface   xi

1 Improving Leadership Ability   1

    What Makes a Good Leader?   1
    The Art of Managing Others   3
    A People Person (On Being One)   4
    Delegation of Authority   5
    General Manager and Managers   6
    Leadership Styles   7
    Systems Approach to Management   12
    Updating Knowledge   14
    References   14

2 Practicing Better Human Relations   16

    The Individual Qualities of Workers   16
    Conflicts and Compromises   20
    Combating Tardiness and Absenteeism   21
    Enjoying Work   21
    What Employees Want from Their Work   22
    Love   24
    Quality of Work Life   24
    Recognition   26
    Titles   27
    Social Intercourse   28
    Smoking   28
    Stress   29
    Thank You   31
    Unions   31
    Firing People (and Those Who Quit)   34
    References   36

3   Developing Communication Skills   37

    Being Understood   37
    Listening   39
    Meetings   43
    Organization Charts and Organization   44
    Policy Manuals   46
    Touring the Premises   48
    References   48
    Bibliography   48

4   Increasing Productivity   49

    Payroll Productivity   49
    Staff Planning and Scheduling   52
    Alternative Work Provisions   57
    Employee's Health, Nutrition and Attitudes   61
    Better Use of Underused People   62
    References   63

5   Selecting Employees   64

    Finding Employees   64
    Interviewing, Selecting Employees and Affirmative Action   66
    Job Analysis   71
    Job Descriptions   71
    Job Specification   72
    Job Evaluation   73
    Job Qualities   75
    Placement   75
    Tests   76
    References   77

6   Training and Supervising Staff   78

    Training, Trainees and Trainers   78
    Educational Upgrading   95
    Evaluating Employees   96
    Supervisors   99
    References   100
    Bibliography   101

7   Motivating Employees   102

    Incentive Programs   102
    Bonuses   109
    Scanlon Plan   110
    Salary and Wage Review   114
    A Compensation Plan   116
    Fringe Benefits   118

Promotion from Within 121
Retirement 121
References 122

8 Avoiding Legal Problems and Losses 123
Respecting Employee's Laws 123
Employee's Insurance 125
Theft Prevention and Security 126
References 145

Appendix A. Selected Job Descriptions 147
Bar and Beverage 148
Dining Room Service 151
Food Preparation 164
Kitchen Operation 180
Office and Building 185

Appendix B. Selected Trade Journals and Book Publishers 189
Foodservice Trade Journals 189
Personnel and Management Trade Journals 190
Addresses of Book Publishers Cited 190

Index 191

Preface

This Book and How to Use It

Presented in this volume you will find the distilled experiences of many successful foodservice managers. These have been blended with practical applications of the psychology of human relations in working situations. The resulting principles have been tried and proven—just like a successful recipe.

As manager, you can implement these suggestions on employee management with confidence. However, be sure that you evaluate the ideas in terms of the size of your foodservice and its special aspects of location, age, type of operation and the competition. Not all of the methods suggested are 100% applicable to all foodservices. But almost all of them are. Be venturesome. Try these methods for a long enough time to make a fair judgment of the results. Chances are good that you will be pleased with these guidelines and be a happier manager as well. Focus your attention and imagination on each of the topics presented. Help your employees to be as productive and fulfilled as they can and deserve to be, and all of you will be the richer.

In the United States, no one is more respected than the successful business owner and manager. Let your employees make you such a person!

You can quickly find any subject in the Contents or Index and read it in a rather short time. Keep the book where it will be handy for reference when you wish advice. Begin by examining the entire book to see what topics are included. Then sample a few of these to become familiar with the methods or suggestions presented. Read the entire book to obtain the full coverage of employee management methods. Jot down the main ideas in a particular section and then discuss these with someone else such as your assistant or supervisor or one of your best employees. If the thoughts expressed seem feasible, sum these up in a memo to yourself. Let it simmer in your mind for a day or so, and then make your decision. Using these suggestions should help make that decision the right one.

Employee Management

The success of any foodservice business depends in great measure upon the attitudes and productivity of its work force. Skilled employees who uphold standards and have a spirit of cooperation, enthusiasm and gracious hospitality are what make the business profit and grow in favor with its customers and patrons. Managers who devote a considerable part of their working time to the various problems of human relations and recognize that personnel functions are of the utmost importance will reap the rewards of having a responsive and productive staff.

Most of the other problems such as sales, food and beverage costs, creating new products, and good public relations have much of their roots in how well the staff responds to training, supervision and management. Thus it is difficult to overemphasize the importance of personnel management.

This book considers the most important aspects of human resources management in the foodservice industry. It outlines the essential elements of good human resource management. Personnel management is concerned with obtaining and maintaining an excellent and satisfied staff of employees. Finding, selecting and placing the right people in the right jobs is seldom an easy job. Providing the supervision and finding the right incentives to keep and hold good employees on the job is even more of a management challenge. This book should be of material help toward meeting that challenge!

The first-rate foodservice manager tries to maximize the productivity of the staff through the application of sound and proven human resources policies and practices. A sensitive manager is fully aware of the human element in reaching the goals that have been set for the organization. Also, personnel management is a never ending responsibility. Employment conditions are constantly changing. Management must be fully aware of these changes and alter procedures accordingly to maintain efficiency and productivity. Thus personnel management requires everyday alertness and awareness in every section or department.

Human resource management is the responsibility of every manager or supervisor. In fact, trends in this field have been toward delegation of the personnel function from the general manager to the department heads and supervisors. Thus, if the supervisor expects to obtain outstanding service from those under him or her, the practice of intelligent personnel management must be kept uppermost in mind and implemented at all times. Study and practice to improve supervisory ability will be necessary for all supervisors and department heads.

Success in personnel management cannot be achieved without good planning. Thus, there must be cooperative planning work between the general manager and all of the supervisory staff and assistants. Creative thinking is needed for all personnel needs and the solutions to workers' problems. This planning effort is just as important as planning for increased sales, working on finance problems, or changing to a new format for the menu. For after all, the employees are the most valuable asset.

The author extends his best wishes for much success in employee management.

Acknowledgments

My sincere appreciation goes to Dr. Lewis J. Minor, Professor, School of Hotel, Restaurant, and Institutional Management at Michigan State University, for his encouragement and assistance in completing this writing, and to Angelos Vlahakis, Robert Herron, and Chef Robert Nelson of the same school for their most helpful advice. My thanks go also to Theodore L. Smith, University Food Services, for his assistance in procuring photographic illustrations.

Robert W. McIntosh

The L. J. Minor
FOODSERVICE STANDARDS SERIES

Lewis J. Minor, Editor

School of Hotel, Restaurant and
  Institutional Management
Michigan State University
East Lansing, Michigan

Volume 1. NUTRITIONAL STANDARDS
         Lewis J. Minor
Volume 2. SANITATION, SAFETY AND ENVIRONMENTAL STANDARDS
         Lewis J. Minor
Volume 3. BASIC ACCOUNTING STANDARDS
         Jack D. Ninemeier and Raymond S. Schmidgall
Volume 4. EMPLOYEE MANAGEMENT STANDARDS
         Robert W. McIntosh

1 Improving Leadership Ability

WHAT MAKES A GOOD LEADER?

Leadership is the key to success in any organization. There are two levels of leaders: supervisors or department heads and the general and assistant managers. Both of these levels perform management functions. Thus, a manager manages a section or a department or the entire business (Pizam 1982).

In a small organization the manager is synonymous with the supervisor. All of the employees are under this particular manager.

Some of the important characteristics of a good leader (Townsend 1970) are as follows.

1. *Accessibility.* The manager should always have an "open door" and be accessible to employees for as many hours in each day as possible.

2. *Knowledge.* The leader should have superior knowledge of all of the technical aspects of managing and operating a foodservice.

3. *Experience.* The manager must be considered as an experienced person who has learned what works and what does not work.

4. *Forward looking outlook.* A good leader has eyes on the future and on improvements that can be made in the operation.

5. *Humility.* Every good leader knows that in a foodservice there are many jobs that employees can do better than he/she can. A good manager recognizes this and gives credit to each employee.

6. *Empathy.* The competent manager tries to look at employee situations from the employee standpoint. The manager places himself/herself in employee situations to attempt to understand the problems.

7. *Firmness.* The manager must have an ability to make decisions, some of which may be rather difficult. Once the decision is made the manager must stick with it. Employees respect a manager who is firm but fair with all the staff.

8. *Approachability.* Each employee should feel that the leader is easily approached and that communications can flow freely between the employee and the leader.

9. *Improvement-minded outlook.* The leader is constantly searching for methods to improve the operation. Nothing is accepted without asking: Could it be done better some other way?

10. *Accommodating attitude.* The manager tries to adjust to the extent possible the policies of the foodservice to the values and needs of employees by reexamining policy to enhance the mutually beneficial relationship.

11. *Goal-oriented outlook.* The leader has specific goals and objectives that are to be met during a certain period. These goals and objectives guide the leader in making decisions and are communicated to employees who can help achieve them (Koppel 1978).

There are two types of leadership behavior patterns:

1. *Supportive behavior.* This term describes the leader as being friendly, approachable, very considerate, positively oriented, and thoughtful of employee needs. It is a participative management style, further described under Leadership Styles in this chapter.

2. *Directive behavior.* This behavior is task-oriented and it is aimed at making clear each employee's roles and tasks both as an individual and as a part of the organizational group. (See the section on Leadership Styles.)

Supportive behavior encourages the group to work together to accomplish a task and it also enhances each individual's feelings of value and self-worth. This helps to motivate them to engage in cooperative behavior which is aimed at achieving organizational goals.

Directive behavior helps clarify for each employee and for the group what they must do in order to make the foodservice successful.

Implementation of these attitudes and policies will produce a much more successful task performance in the foodservice business.

One of the most effective leadership styles is to outwardly show a genuine interest in each and every employee. The manager or assistant manager spends some time every day with every employee. It might be for just a few minutes or even seconds, for a cordial greeting. But this practice clearly shows the employees that the managers really care about them and are there to be of help and support whenever they might be needed. Such contact gives the employees the opportunity to speak to the manager and if something is bothering them or they need some assistance or advice, the opportunity is there every day for them to obtain help. Another benefit that arises from this particular leadership practice is that pride in work and in the organization begins to build up. For example, if someone should ask an employee if this foodservice is a good place to eat, the reply might well be, "It's the best restaurant in this part of the country! Try it and see for yourself!" This attitude comes about when the manager teaches all staff members how important their support is to the organization's success.

THE ART OF MANAGING OTHERS

The management of people is both a science and an art (Nebel 1978). Like any other worthwhile skill or profession, being a manager requires practice and study. It is one thing to know the intricacies of the foodservice business but it is quite another to know how to direct and supervise employees in performing the tasks necessary for a successful operation.

The *science of management* applies principally to the interpretation of financial reports and other types of reports; it involves compliance with various laws and regulations that affect the business. To this should be added the science of food receiving, storage, issuance, preparation and service to the customer as well as the science of ordering food and beverages in the most advantageous manner.

The *art of management* comprises the interpretation which the manager makes of any situation presenting itself and the skill which is used by the manager to solve that particular problem. Developing these skills is an art. They are only accomplished and achieved by experience and by studying journal articles (e.g., Nebel and Stearns 1977) and books such as this one and those by Axler (1979) and Morgan (1981). New ideas arise by attending conferences, food shows, seminars, short courses and conventions where new methods are taught.

The application of good common sense is an important ingredient. Like any art, practice makes perfect. Any application of good management principles in practical situations will provide the practice and experience that are needed in order to be an artful, effective manager. As a practical matter, it probably takes about 3 years for anyone to achieve the expertness needed to successfully manage a moderate-sized foodservice.

A PEOPLE PERSON (ON BEING ONE)

There is no business any more concerned with people than the foodservice business. In fact, some of the best and worst qualities of people seem to be brought out when they are guests in an eating place. Eating out is a psychological experience as well as a physiological necessity. A highly successful restaurateur once remarked that about 60% of the satisfaction of dining in a restaurant has nothing whatsoever to do with food. Such a comment implies emphasis on the importance of service, decor, atmosphere, politeness, physical comfort, and probably other considerations such as linen, china, silver, glass, and furnishings.

Foodservice managers have three publics—their own staff, their customers, and the other business people in their community. Thus, a manager must be a people person to the utmost degree. Developing ability to manage people and to deal with people can be enhanced in several ways. One method is to enroll in a Dale Carnegie course which emphasizes the skills and abilities needed to be a better people person. Another is concentrated practice in applied psychology in a business situation. Numerous books and articles are available that provide guidance. (See Appendix B.) The other facet of improving one's ability is practice. Like playing the piano, practicing is absolutely essential to improve ability.

The manager must spend some time with the guests and try to learn their names. No other technique is so effective in building relationships with customers. These customers will talk to their friends who will be attracted to the foodservice because of word-of-mouth advertising on the part of these satisfied customers. Wearing a name tag, which is clearly and easily read, is one way to help to identify yourself with your guests. Employees should also wear name tags, preferably the plastic type which has large clear letters that are easily read by the customers and fellow workers. Of course, the managers must be sure they know the full name of every employee.

Each employee should feel perfectly free to talk to the manager or his/her supervisor at any time. A manager cannot be a good people person unless he/she is accessible to the staff in an easy, informal manner. If any employee has a suggestion, it should always be carefully considered. The manager can write the idea down and then study it further when time permits. If the idea is accepted and put into practice, some kind of reward should be offered to the giver of the suggestion. If it is not accepted, the employee should be given a subsequent explanation as to why the idea was not implemented.

One final thought on being a people person is the importance of being consistent. This means not changing direction in the middle of the stream and not making last minute changes and alternations in agreed upon plans. Also, if a promise is made to do something, it is necessary to follow through and do it. Nothing is more demoralizing or disappointing than to be told by the manager that something is going to happen or to have the manager promise to do something and then to never see it happen or get done.

DELEGATION OF AUTHORITY

The difference between authority and responsibility should be noted. *Authority* is the right to give directions, take action, make final decisions, or have jurisdiction over a certain matter. On the other hand, *responsibility* is the condition or quality of being responsible, or being answerable, or having been personally delegated some particular duty.

So to make things happen, it is extremely important for a manager to increase productivity by delegating authority. One of the biggest problems in many foodservices is that there is insufficient delegation of authority. Often decisions may be made more quickly and advantageously if authority has been delegated.

With the definitions in mind, it is important to remember that when authority is delegated, responsibility must also be delegated. However, the manager has the ultimate responsibility for the entire foodservice operation and its performance. Thus, *ultimate* responsibility and authority cannot be delegated.

A good rule when delegating authority is to be sure that this authority is well understood (Morgan 1979). The person should be held responsible for those elements of authority that have been so delegated. Authority and responsibility must go together. Responsibility should not be delegated without the appropriate delegation of authority to carry these matters to their proper conclusion. The trend in business today is to delegate as much responsibility and authority as possible. Delegating this authority to supervisors and department heads is a wise method of reducing the manager's burdens (Guyette 1981). But remember, when authority is delegated so is responsibility and vice versa. For example, if one delegates the responsibility of personnel matters to the department head or supervisors, one must be sure to also give them the authority to take all necessary action. They should be reminded that they will be responsible for any problems that their particular personnel decisions cause. If they hire the wrong person, they can only blame themselves and suffer the consequences.

In turn, department heads and supervisors should delegate as much authority and responsibility to each of their employees as possible. So doing increases each employee's sense of importance and responsibility and improves the overall productivity of the organization. The rule is *delegate as much as possible at all levels of the organization.*

GENERAL MANAGER AND MANAGERS

In a sense, every employee of a foodservice operation is a manager (Lane 1976). Each employee has a particular assignment and must manage this assignment adequately. Therefore this job must be performed in a manner that contributes to the overall goals and schedules of the organization. Thus, every employee should be considered a manager of sorts.

In the more formal sense, the general or overall manager of the entire organization is the manager. But each of the department heads or supervisors is also a manager. These people are just as much managers of their own departments as is the manager of the foodservice or other restaurant enterprise. When one speaks of managers one actually means at least all of the supervisors and department heads and the assistant and general manager. But, really, every employee is a manager in the sense that he/she must competently manage his/her own job.

The success of any business organization is a direct reflection of the competency and performance of the general manager. This manager is a "role model." Everyone who works under this manager looks to the manager as a model or ideal which sets the standard for the entire operation. Employees are very quick to recognize various qualities in their manager or supervisor. If weaknesses are discovered, then these weaknesses are sometimes used by the employees as an excuse for not doing their jobs properly. For example, a new manager who knows very little about training has been assigned to a foodservice. As a consequence, these employees are not going to be very well trained. Or, if the manager is careless about personal appearance, employees are likewise prone to have standards somewhat similar for personal appearance. It is important that the manager, regardless of what kind, know intimately every detail of the job and the proper standards to be adhered to regarding that job. The manager cannot know too much. The more familiar the manager is with every conceivable aspect of the operation, the more respect the manager will receive from the employees and the better the job will be done by the foodservice enterprise.

Self-Discipline

Perceptive students and practitioners of the art and science of management believe that about 95% of the success of a manager is self-discipline. If the manager can manage himself/herself, the business will be well managed.

Bottoms-Up Management

An interesting philosophy relating to management is that it is management's primary duty to support the subordinate managers and their staffs. In other words, the manager's main job is to do whatever is necessary to help and teach the staff to give superb service to the guests and produce the products that are the most appealing and tasty. The manager constantly gives recognition and respect for jobs well done. The employees are the ones in contact with the guests and customers. Therefore, the impression that these guests have of the business is made primarily by the employees. The employee is thus the center of management's attention. This being true, the customers should receive the best possible service and the most satisfying products from the employees. These statements should not imply that the manager should have no contact with the customers and guests. Some of the most successful foodservices have managers who make a real effort to spend part of every working day with their guests, as well as with each of their employees. So doing builds wonderful guest relations, and word-of-mouth advertising is the best and cheapest kind. Thus, this effort is time well spent.

Team Approach

An excellent philosophy for a manager is that of a "team approach." If each employee sees himself/herself as a member of the foodservice "team" and knows what the goal is of that particular organization at any time, the likelihood of success is much more probable than would be the case when each employee is simply performing the job as directed. A football team knows its exact objective—to move the ball across the goal line. The team wants to do this as many times as possible during the period of the game. Using this same comparison, each employee of the foodservice should know exactly what the goals are and do his/her utmost to help the "team" achieve its goals. There must be a known reward at the other end so that the employee understands what the gains will be if the goals are achieved. But that is another subject to be taken up under "incentives." (See Chapter 7.)

LEADERSHIP STYLES

Some flexibility is needed in management styles to meet the needs of each particular circumstance. For example, in a manager's relationships with other managers—department heads and supervisors—a different management style is used than in dealing with a new employee or an emergency situation. There are many other considerations here. Management style in each situation depends on the manager's policy of what is the most sensible, yet effective manner of dealing with the situation. The following discussion is intended to clarify the two foundational philosophies of management including the widely recognized theories of McGregor (1944).

Generally, *participative management* is the best style since it is thought to be the most effective in the majority of situations. However, there are specific and extreme situations in which *task-oriented leadership style* is best.

Participative Management Style

A participative-type management style works best in a moderate situation. A good example would be the planning of next year's advertising program. One of the assistant managers or another staff member may have a real talent for advertising. Such a person can be very helpful in discussing these plans and in contributing ideas about how much the budget should be and how the funds can be most effectively spent. In this situation, the manager works with this staff member to create the advertising plan. The same principle applies in any other situation in which the manager participates with associates so that they can contribute to the soundness of the decisions being made. This management style has an additional advantage in that the overall success of the foodservice becomes a combination of direction, participation, and inspiration. The successful general manager supplies all three. The degree to which this is supplied will determine the manager's satisfaction and that of the employees, customers, and owners (Nebel 1978.) These concepts illustrate supportive leadership behavior as previously described (in the section What Makes a Good Leader?) and demonstrate application of McGregor's theory Y.

McGregor's Theory Y

The theory Y leader is a true believer in staff participation (see McGregor 1944). This belief is founded on the assumption that subordinates already possess motivation. They will seek out responsibility and do their jobs. The theory Y manager is people oriented in leadership style and attempts to involve subordinates in making decisions. This is done in the belief that morale will be raised and the entire operation will be improved. Because subordinates want to do a good job, they will be willing and able to improve productivity.

McGregor found that individuals with independent-type personalities respond favorably to invitations to participate actively in decision making. The use of theory Y management style is the most effective with such employees who show an interest in the business. If theory Y is attempted with employees who are not so constituted, the effectiveness of the manager will be less.

Another good example of using theory Y would be creating an employee incentive plan. Members of the staff could provide valuable input as to what kind of plan would produce the best results.

Management trends today are very much in the direction of theory Y. Participative management style, as much as possible, tends to create a better feeling between all of the employees and the management. This is especially so if employees are more educated and are more capable, hard working types (Simmons and Mares 1983).

Task-Oriented Management Style

Teaching a beginning worker about the dish machine and how to operate it requires a task-oriented leadership style. The manager knows how to operate the machine, the employee nothing about it. Since participative style is not appropriate, the manager teaches the operation by doing it.

Likewise, in a very difficult situation, the task-oriented method can be best. For example, if there is suddenly a grease fire in the kitchen, the immediate task is to put out the fire. Task-oriented leadership would be exemplified by a chef who immediately rushes to the site of the fire and extinguishes it.

McGregor's Theory X

The theory X manager tends to be bossy and operates on the assumption that the staff is passive and not very interested in the needs of the organization. Therefore, all employees need a lot of direction and motivation. This management style declares that the manager makes all the decisions and the orders are issued down to the workers. Two professors at the School of Hotel, Restaurant, and Tourism Administration at the University of New Orleans have termed this style "task-oriented leadership" (Nebel and Stearns 1977). Their research indicates that theory X leadership style is effective when the manager is confronted by either a very easy or a very difficult leadership situation. It follows that the simpler (or more difficult) the job the more likely the task-oriented style will be the best.

Also, the workers will be more likely to accept the leader's authority if there is a very good relationship. The other factor is position power. This is the degree to which the leader has the authority to reward or punish workers. The greater this power the more influence the leader will have on the subordinates.

Thus, task-oriented leaders (theory X) are the most forceful in favorable situations where there are good leader−subordinate relations. Also, they are most effectual when there are structured tasks to be performed and a strong leader position of power. Furthermore, the theory X leadership style is the most effective in unfavorable situations, where there are poor leader—subordinate relations, unstructured tasks, and a very weak power position. So, if the manager is a very strong leader and very well supported by subordinates or if he/she is a very weak leader with not much support from subordinates, then using the theory X, dominating, autocratic style would work the best. Regarding the work, if the task is very simple such as instructions on mopping the floor for a beginning employee or the task is extremely difficult such as preparing a complex cost report to your board of directors, then the theory X leadership style would be best.

Summary and Suggestion

In either an extremely difficult or an easy task structure with excellent manager—subordinate relations and strong position power *or* a difficult task structure with weak position power, theory X is the best to use. All situations between these two extremes are favorable to the application of theory Y. Thus, whether or not a particular leadership style will be effective depends upon the situation variables surrounding the work group and the personality traits of the members of that group.

A good suggestion is to write down a list of the main tasks that a manager performs. Then opposite each of these tasks, indicate whether theory X or theory Y would be most effective. Such an exercise should prove to be a useful method of increasing managerial perceptions and understanding. It also is a good starting point from which to refine the applications of these leadership styles and improve managerial ability and effectiveness.

Japanese Theory Z

One concept of this theory is that the manager uses the so-called *larger interlocking authority*. What this means is that decisions are made on the front line—on the floor where the problems exist. They are made on the basis of wisdom and expertise by those who are directly confronting the problem. The theory is very strong on communications. The managers and their employees are constantly involved in helping to make decisions, and everybody in the organization puts in their best ideas. Each manager works with all of the involved employees—on any one particular problem—to reach the best solution, and everyone considers the same aspects of the same problem. This method is probably the ultimate in employee involvement in decision making (Ouchi 1981).

For example, suppose there is a new dish machine needed. The steps that the Z-type manager would take is to include everyone who has any relationship whatsoever with the dish machine in planning for a new one. This would first necessitate a meeting to which all involved personnel are invited (see Fig. 1). Those interested would come and all of their ideas on this matter would contribute to the solution of the problem of installing the new dish machine. Everyone would be thinking along the same lines about the same problem to reach the best solution. These ideas would be collected and organized by the kitchen steward, who draws up the resulting plans that determine which dish machine is selected and how it is installed. This method gives a part in the planning processes to all of the employees who are involved and interested in having a better dish machine. They each have ample opportunity to contribute their ideas on what kind of a dish washing machine should be ordered and how it will be installed. The end result should be a far more satisfactory dish machine that is better located and functions better and with higher productivity than would have been the case had the steward simply decided independently on the details of the new machine and had it installed.

Meetings

Under the Z management theory the general manager has a meeting with all subsidiary managers at least once a week. During this meeting common problems are discussed and their solutions are considered. *Involvement* is the key word and the guiding theme of the general manager's art of management. It works. One need only try it.

FIG. 1. Theory Z in action. Department head discusses proposed improvements and new equipment with staff. Involvement of each member is a key to good morale and motivation. *Courtesy of Michigan State University Foodservice*

SYSTEMS APPROACH TO MANAGEMENT

In *systems approach management*, the manager looks at the business or organization as a totally interrelated entity with various parts that all fit together, mutually reinforcing each other as a system to produce the desired outcome.

By contrast, a *hierarchical approach to business* looks at the organization from the standpoint of who is the manager and who are the supervisors and who are the workers: who reports to whom and who is under whom and who is over whom in the graded ranks.

The systems approach requires three major components: (1) the resource variables, (2) the operational variables, and (3) the goals.

Resource Variables

The resource variables of the foodservice organization involve people, materials, money and information—the basics which the manager has at command. Consider that these resources are (1) the people who are the workers, (2) all of the materials, supplies, equipment, tools, and real estate used by these people, (3) the money and capital that the manager has available in terms of funds, equity, and borrowing capacity, and (4) the information that the manager needs every day in order to make the best marketing, production, and financial decisions. These four resource groups relate to each other, but they likewise are intimately related to the operational variables.

Operational Variables

Human behavior, time and change are the operational variables. These are manipulated by the manager. How human behavior maximizes results is studied diligently by the manager. These should be related to the use of time, scheduling, productivity, the passage of time, obsolescence and the management of change. All of these are closely interrelated and are utilized to their best advantage to produce the short- and long-range goals that have been established for the organization.

Thinking about the systems approach to management is a productive exercise. These interrelationships become more clear when studied. A smart manager, who tries to clearly identify the qualities that are needed for the systems approach to be better understood, will conclude that the most important factors are communication, interpersonal relationships, goal setting, and enthusiastic cooperation of all of the staff. Everyone tries to move the business towards the goals and thus to produce the desired results. Figure 2 illustrates these relationships.

Goals

Maximization of resource utilization is the overall goal established for the organization. Goals should have two characteristics: They should be (a) measurable and (b) reasonable and attainable.

An example of a long-term goal is for the foodservice to achieve a 15% net profit return on invested capital. Or a short-term goal might be a 10% increase in gross dollar volume compared with last year. Another example would be to set as a goal a certain figure representing the desired net profit for a particular year, or a specific reduction in waste or costs.

But goals must have that second quality of being reasonable. It is not rational to set goals far higher than is likely to be achieved.

The Main Idea

Looking at a business organization from the systems approach is advantageous. The manager thinks of the resource variables, the operational variables, and the goals in terms of how each part of the business can provide a maximum contribution to the other parts. All of the parts are systematized

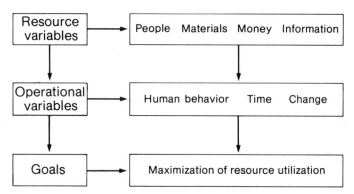

FIG. 2. Systems approach to foodservice management. *Comments*: This system emphasizes the common goal of the entire organization's makeup. It accentuates the need for common dedication, communication, mutual assistance among all workers, and full utilization of all the resources at the command of the general manager. It deemphasizes who is over whom and who reports to whom or other hierarchal implications. The systems approach also relates to the theory Y management style (see McGregor's Theory Y in this chapter).

together to achieve the total goals. Looking at the business in this way, the manager thinks of each of the departments or sections as being part of a system which is totally interrelated to produce the desired results.

UPDATING KNOWLEDGE

It is important to utilize every feasible opportunity to improve understanding and knowledge of the business. One learns as long as one lives and the more open-minded the person, the better able to guide the foodservice into ever-growing successes. Also, self-education and continuing education help to avoid some of the problems and to handle unusual difficulties when they come along.

Reading the various trade journals (see Appendix B) is probably the most feasible method by which a manager updates his/her knowledge. Attendance at trade shows and educational forums likewise is a valuable method. Participating in workshops and seminars that are sponsored by the National Restaurant Association and other national and state trade groups invariably produces usable ideas that become valuable tools in improving management. Hiring consultants from time to time who are specialists in a particular phase of the business is another good way to build management ability. Consultants are usually up to the minute on trends and concepts within their special field and they can be helpful to the manager in many different ways.

Occasionally taking a trip and participating as a customer at various restaurants and other types of foodservices is broadening and a source of useful ideas. Talking with managers in different parts of the country and in foreign countries adds considerably to understanding and appreciation of the business and the myriad of combinations of ways in which foodservices can become more successful and satisfying. Being a foodservice manager is a very demanding and responsible job. Efforts to become better educated and more knowledgeable will pay off in improvements to the foodservice as well as making the job more pleasurable and professionally fulfilling.

REFERENCES

AXLER, B.H. 1979. Foodservice: A Managerial Approach. D.C. Heath and Co., Lexington, MA.
GUYETTE, W.C. 1981. The executive chef: Manager or culinarian? The Cornell Hotel and Restaurant Administration Quarterly 22, 71–76.
KOPPEL, J.N. 1978. The food service manager of the future. The Cornell Hotel and Restaurant Administration Quarterly 19, 36–39.

LANE, H.E. 1976. The Scanlon Plan: A key to productivity and payroll costs. The Cornell Hotel and Restaurant Administration Quarterly *17*, 76–80.

McGREGOR, D. 1944. Getting effective leadership in an industrial organization. Advanced Management *9*, 148–153.

MORGAN, W.J. 1979. Hospitality Personnel Management. CBI Publishing Co., Boston, MA.

MORGAN, W.J. 1981. Food and Beverage Management and Science. Educational Institute, American Hotel and Motel Association, East Lansing, MI.

NEBEL, E.C. 1978. Motivation, leadership, and employee performance: A review. The Cornell Hotel and Restaurant Administration Quarterly *19*, 62–69.

NEBEL, E.C. and STEARNS, G.K. 1977. Leadership in the hospitality industry. The Cornell Hotel and Restaurant Administration Quarterly *18*, 69–76.

OUCHI, W. 1981. Theory Z How American Business Can Meet the Japanese Challenge. Addison-Wesley Publishing Co. Reading, MA.

PIZAM, A. 1982. The Practice of Hospitality Management. AVI Publishing Co., Westport, CT.

SIMMONS, J. and MARES, W. 1983. Working Together. Alfred Knopf, New York, NY.

TOWNSEND, R. 1970. Up the Organization. Alfred Knopf, New York, NY.

 Practicing Better
Human Relations

THE INDIVIDUAL QUALITIES OF WORKERS

Everyone is alike—yet everyone is different. But, as a manager, it is very important to recognize that there are certain qualities within the employees that are very important when these workers react to the requirements of their employment. Among the most significant of these qualities are the employee's needs, values, perceptions of the job, and expectations of what the job will do for them. Also important are their motivation to work for the organization, their native abilities, performance on the job, the satisfactions derived from their work, the pleasures of the workplace for them, and possibly the stress they may develop over certain aspects of their work.

Needs of Employees

Needs refer to those requirements for physical well being such as physical needs of the body and the psychological or mental needs. An employee may not be entirely aware of all of these needs, but they are needs nevertheless.

As manager, some of the needs of staff that must be considered are as follows:

1. Need for food, beverages, and bodily comfort
2. Physical safety and freedom from health hazards
3. Inspiration and leadership from supervisor and manager

4. Achievement—to accomplish something worthwhile
5. Direction and help when needed to do a very good job
6. Knowledge of the results of work—especially good reports on their work
7. Fairness of treatment
8. Recognition of worth and some degree of status
9. Acceptance by fellow workers and customers
10. Self-esteem
11. A feeling of being responsible
12. Upright conduct
13. Security and predictability
14. Consistent policies of supervisor and manager

The employee's performance on the job and attitude about the job will depend on the degree to which the manager fulfills these needs (Nebel 1978). Conversely, the employee's performance and attitude toward the job will be strongly affected by the degree of absence of the fulfillment of these needs.

If employees do work under conditions of serious lack of need fulfillment, then, in attempting to gain a higher degree of self-possession, they will deliberately do bad work, steal and even damage some equipment, dishes or supplies. Thus, it pays a manager to listen to the employees and conscientiously try to satisfy their needs to the extent possible.

Employee Values

Values are the importance that each person places on such diverse matters as physical objects, other people, activities, behavior and even thoughts. The values of one person might be much different than another's. For example, a loaf of bread is vastly more valuable to a starving man than to another man who has just finished a large steak dinner. Yet the bread would cost the same to either man. Thus values exist only to the degree that the individual person evaluates that particular item or whatever else is being valued. The employee's performance on the job is importantly affected by his/her values (Schuler 1981). If the manager is to do a good job with the employees, then it is important to know what each employee values most. Actually, values may influence an employee's performance more than needs, as part of these needs may be of a subconscious nature while values are ever present in the employee's mind. Here again, it is advantageous to the manager to learn as much as possible about the values held by each employee. So doing then makes the management job more effective. A manager who knows what the employee's values are can then create the outcomes that come as close as possible to what the employee values.

For example, suppose that a manager discovers that one of the employees is very interested in accumulating tangible goods or property. This employee believes that if something is to be worthwhile, it has to be useful. Such a person will readily accept a special training program because of the expected reward—a higher paying job. Such incentives as bonuses, profit sharing, merit raises, and promotions based on outstanding performance have a tremendous appeal to this employee. By contrast, a new pension plan effective at age 70 would have a very limited appeal.

Another example might be someone who is quite sensitive and has a great interest in beauty and nature. This person has a great appreciation for art, poetry, and music. Often a person of this type loves to share aesthetic experiences with others and is usually a good communicator. Such a person very likely has excellent taste in clothes and other possessions. This person would excel as dining room hostess or maître d' or captain.

An employee may put great value on helping people. This type of person is concerned about the welfare of others and would be a good type to do training in the foodservice. Also, this kind of person would be an excellent waiter or waitress, who gets great satisfaction from helping others to enjoy their meal and feels a love for fellow man.

Still another kind of person is one who puts a high value on power over others. Titles may be even more important than money. Psychic income such as recognition and pats on the back mean a great deal. A person of this kind seeks promotion to manager and even higher positions if the hierarchy is so constituted.

Some others have a deep sense of morality and are very respectful of their supervisors and managers. They like standard ways of doing things and expect others to be respectful and cooperative. They do not respond particularly well to incentives related to more pay, bonuses, or more authority for themselves.

One last type of person places very high value on learning things. This kind of person is primarily interested in the pursuit and accumulation of knowledge. Such a person particularly likes training programs, self-study courses, meetings, and discussions with supervisors and fellow workers on how a particular problem might be solved. The person likes to study a problem and consider various possibilities for resolving the situation. This person tends to be critical of others, nonemotional, piercing, acute and impatient with people who use numerous generalizations.

Two more important thoughts about values: (1) Values change during a person's life—a value which is of the utmost importance at one period of life may become much diminished and have another take its place. (2) Everyone possesses all of the main values at the same time, but it is the *relative* importance of each which is of the most concern to an employee's supervisor or manager. What is the individual's most important value? Talking and carefully listening to each employee brings these relative values to light.

A manager who makes sufficient effort to learn about the values of staff members is thus well equipped to evaluate the kind of relationships that provide optimal satisfaction to the employee from his/her work (Sargent 1981). At the same time this manager is procuring for the foodservice the optimum services of each employee. This maximizes the contribution that each employee makes to the success of the organization.

Perceptions and Expectations of the Job

Each employee will look at the job from his/her own individual viewpoint. One employee, for example, perceives the job as simply a means to an end—a necessity in order to earn the means to achieve a college education. For another, it is a necessity in order to earn a living. A newly graduated restaurant management major sees the job as a first step towards ultimately managing or owning a certain type of foodservice establishment. Someone else might look at the job as an opportunity to begin rising up the ladder to ever more responsibilities and to higher paying positions within this organization. Another may view the job as a great opportunity to learn new skills and abilities which will open the doors to new opportunities in the future.

Ability of Employees

The employee's ability consists of two parts—aptitudes and skill. Aptitude refers to a person's potential to accomplish something or master a concept or idea. Skill means the actual ability to master an idea or do something at the present time. Aptitudes are important as they indicate the degree to which this person will adjust to a new situation in the foodservice and to new methods, concepts, and environments. The demands of some jobs may change in time, and thus the worker's aptitudes are very important. If the job is not likely to do much changing, skills are indeed of utmost importance.

Performance on the Job

The actual job performance expresses the end result of all of the employee's qualities as they relate to the job. This is the ultimate expression of how all of the employee's qualities respond to the direction of supervisory management. *Skilled management should produce exemplary performance.*

Employee Satisfaction

For employees to be satisfied they must feel that they are performing well. It is their level of performance that brings this about. They can also be satisfied by the performance of the group in which they work. If the group's performance is good to excellent, an individual in the group feels satisfaction.

Receiving pay is satisfying, but the best pay system closely ties compensation to performance. Those who do not perform well do not receive as much pay. Therefore, those who work hard and perform well reap the benefits of their work and receive the resulting satisfaction of higher pay. Many people would rather work harder, take on more responsibility, and receive the satisfaction of earning a high salary or hourly rate. This gives them much satisfaction.

By contrast, employees can perform well, but still be dissatisfied. Such a situation is more typical of short-run conditions than for the long pull. Employees may resent certain aspects of their job including their pay, but because they like the job and are hoping for an improvement in the future, they continue to perform well under these conditions.

The goal for the manager or supervisor is to try to achieve both employee satisfaction and good performance. This can be accomplished with determination and application of exemplary human resource management tempered by experience and the mistakes made along the way (Wasmuth and Davis 1983).

Pleasures and Stresses of the Workplace

Deriving pleasure from the job should be a common working condition and a plus if it can be increased in a positive way. By contrast, jobs also can produce stress. (See the section in this chapter on Stress.) Helping the employee to cope with stress when it arises and to eliminate causes of stress are productive management efforts.

CONFLICTS AND COMPROMISES

Differences among staff members are bound to appear and can usually be resolved. The manager should listen to both sides carefully and strive to avoid prejudice. Being fair is a basic virtue. If a conflict is really a clash of personalities, then a reassignment of one or the other is likely to be necessary.

Compromises are typically bad management. It is much better to listen to the two contenders and then decide in favor of one (Townsend 1970). This puts the responsibility on the winner to make it work. If a manager gives in, he/she should give in all the way so that the ultimate responsibility for the success of this decision rests squarely on the manager. The staff should be taught to win some skirmishes and lose others like good sports. Each manager and supervisor should have a fair share of victories, however. The department heads should be asked to keep a close watch for conflicts. The cause should be immediately determined and corrective action taken, if possible. If a resolution is not forthcoming, the manager takes the responsibility of settling the matter.

COMBATING TARDINESS AND ABSENTEEISM

Hiring the right kind of people in the first place is the most effective way to minimize this problem. However, these difficulties exist in most operations and a plan to minimize them is good management.

A manager should keep records of instances of tardiness and absenteeism. If they become excessive, there is no other solution than to fire the individual. But the records are important in case the person files for unemployment benefits and the bureau inquires about the reasons why the person was fired.

At the outset of employment, the policy manual clearly shows that the foodservice operation expects each employee to honor his/her schedule and to be present when needed. There is also an explanation of the penalties that will be imposed if infractions occur. In the initial indoctrination of the new employee, the importance and urgency of the need to be prompt should be brought out and emphasized. The intensity of feeling on this matter expressed by the manager will impress upon the new employee its vital importance. Tardiness shows a lack of respect for fellow workers and for the management team. It is also a clear indication of the lack of dependability. There may occasionally be a very valid reason why tardiness or absenteeism occurs. But it is very difficult for a supervisor to sort out the validity of these reasons from just plain "I don't care." So, most supervisors assume that the reasons are not altogether valid and genuine. Sometimes an employee is consistently late. There may indeed be a valid reason and thus, a rescheduling to better accommodate this worker would be mutually advantageous.

Penalties vary but one idea is to see to it that the tardy employee ends up doing the less desirable jobs such as clean up projects or side work. These can be agreed upon by each department. Peer pressure will be quite effective in keeping employees prompt and on the job. Each employee should be fully aware of the consequences of being late or tardy and accept the notations in his or her employment record and the less desirable job assignments.

ENJOYING WORK

Nothing succeeds like success! Success has a way of building upon each achievement making everybody who contributed to this attainment feel happy and satisfied about the degree of success accomplished. One way to say this is "To enjoy your work, do the right thing at the right time and stay out of trouble!"

To be successful in any type of work requires a large degree of pleasure and satisfaction from the work being done. How is this achieved? Intelligent selection, training, placement, and subsequent management of each employee is one of the most important answers. An employee is not going to enjoy work if it is not the type of job that he/she finds suitable and satisfying. There are such wide variations in employees interests, values, abilities, perceptions, intelligence and personalities that there is a real challenge to management to try to make everybody enjoy their work as much as possible.

There is one precaution: The happy, contented employee is not necessarily the most productive. Thus, although it is important that employees be made as satisfied and happy in their jobs as possible, this truth must be recognized. There may be some people who are very productive on the job and are good employees but they simply just are not very happy or satisfied with their work. Ultimately they may leave the organization. But, all attempts to improve their attitude on the job should be made, recognizing that it is not likely that one can be wholly successful in keeping all of the employees enjoying their work.

WHAT EMPLOYEES WANT FROM THEIR WORK

There is only one way to find out what an employee wants from his/her work. This is to talk to the employee in a sincere confident way. The employee should know that the manager is most interested in doing everything possible to make the employee's work as satisfying and meaningful as practicable. Every employee has a strong sense of individuality. The employee wants to express his/her free will and meet personal needs. Thus, in order to identify these, it is necessary to pinpoint the conversation directly to this particular employee's interests. Such procedure leads the employee to attach an even greater importance to the fact that he/she is a unique individual and is an important part of the manager's operational team. When so recognized, each employee then becomes a better member of the working group.

Much of the work satisfaction that is achieved is gained from the social standing awarded to this individual by the working group. An employee has a feeling of belonging and derives satisfactions from the associations that are made within the work group.

Another important consideration is that the employee identifies success with the success of the organization. If the foodservice is successful, the employee then also feels successful because of his/her contributions to that success. Incidentally, management should be sure to impress on each employee at the very outset that this situation is indeed true and that each individual's contribution to the foodservice is important in order to achieve success for all.

Specific Wants

Listed below are some of the most common basic satisfactions and wants that employees desire from their work:

1. *Self-importance.* They want to feel that they are doing something worthwhile and that the work is interesting, useful and varied.

2. *Respect for superiors.* The employees want to be able to trust their supervisor and manager. The manager must have earned the support of the employees and the employees look up to the manager as a good leader.

3. *Part of a team effort.* The employees want to do their share of important work and have the feeling that others depend on them for getting the job done. The employees want to feel that they count for something and have recognition. They want to feel that their special skills and ideas are utilized and that they get credit for good work. They want to know where to go for help when it is needed.

4. *Good wages.* The employees want fair and adequate wages. Also, the wages should be the correct amount or seem correct for the type and level of job the employee does. The employee does not want to feel that he/she is being underpaid for the work that is being performed.

5. *Opportunity for advancement.* The opportunity to get ahead and to prove ability is also important. An employee likes to feel progress and see the opportunity for advancement.

6. *Secure future.* The employees want a safe future and expect a reasonably steady, safe job that hopefully will not terminate. The employees want to know the rules of the job and that they can handle them in a satisfactory manner. Each employee wants to know what is happening in the business and to have good communication from the supervisor or department head and manager.

7. *Self-respect.* Each employee likes to know where he or she fits in, why various events are happening, and that their complaints and ideas are listened to and taken seriously.

8. *Enjoyable working conditions.* Good working conditions are desired with tools and equipment that are in proper condition and that operate perfectly and that are well maintained, clean, and pleasant to use. The employees like to enjoy their work and feel relaxed and happy on the job.

Providing these conditions becomes a substantial challenge to managers at all levels. Usually such a challenge is a continual one and good managers constantly strive to improve the working satisfactions for all.

LOVE

"What the world needs now is love, sweet love." While a foodservice establishment is not a "love boat" there are lots of opportunities to express warm affection and love for and by each person on the staff and especially by the manager. One very successful motel manager kisses his cook every morning. This may appear to be "far out" for some managers, but nevertheless, the fact remains that the cook really feels appreciated. The cook happens to be a female and the manager a male. But it should not matter if it were the other way around. The affection is "purely professional" and illustrates a need for warm affection and feeling among members of the foodservice organization.

Doing little things for each staff member on particular occasions or sending a card when they are ill or showing other expressions of concern and affection is one of the best ways of building a responsive, productive team. An affectionate attitude on the part of the manager for each staff member goes a long way toward building a truly responsive group of employees. Employees will do more if they feel appreciated. They will respond to kind treatment, consideration and manifestations of affection. However, the manager will have to give them outward expressions of appreciation in the form of some kind of communication. This is so that the employee is aware of the fact that the manager does appreciate the individual's efforts and contributions to the success of the organization.

Frank Capra, the famous movie director, recently stated that his success was founded on two principles: the love of people and the recognition as an individual of each person working under his direction. Surely these principles apply to any organization, but particularly to the foodservice business which is so people oriented.

QUALITY OF WORK LIFE

Quality of work life can be defined as the degree to which the employees are able to satisfy their important personal needs and values through their work. The quality of a person's work life should improve as more and more needed values are satisfied by that individual's job and career progression.

People differ considerably. What is important to some is not important to others. Thus, some have considerably different needs than others. A manager who wishes to improve the quality of work life should begin with a private conference with each employee—individually to determine what aspects of the work situation are the most important to that individual. The manager should ask what degree of importance the employee places on various aspects of his/her work.

For example, when hiring a cook the manager could ask, "How important is it to you to learn how to make special gourmet dishes?" Then the manager can make an evaluation of these important needs and how well they are being or could be satisfied by the job. After this evaluation and assessment, the next step is to formulate a course of action to improve the quality of work life. It is important to increase the level of satisfaction of these important needs and values for each individual. This is recognition on the part of the manager that a foodservice organization *can* serve as a source of satisfaction of each employee's needs.

Employees are sometimes unhappy with their jobs and demand more meaningful work (Wasmuth and Davis 1983). This is particularly true of younger employees who are looking at the food industry as a career. Such workers are beginning to demand improvements in both economic and noneconomic outcomes from their jobs. Generally speaking, the importance of nonfinancial rewards is increasing relative to the financial ones. This is especially true among those younger workers who are quite highly educated and have or are seeking professional-type jobs. There is a need for improvement and room for improvement in quality of work life in virtually every foodservice organization.

Ways to Improve Quality of Work Life

Following is a list of techniques that should be considered when improving the quality of work life among a staff. The selection of these, of course, will depend on each individual's particular situation. Also, one must determine which technique would be best applied to assist the employee in achieving a higher quality of work life.

1. Job design
2. Job rotation
3. Job enlargement (adding activities to the employee's job)
4. Job enrichment (supplying the employee's need for more responsibility and opportunity for additional achievement)
5. Participation in decision making

6. Equal treatment of women and minorities for upgraded compensation and promotion
7. Standards for individual job performance
8. Effective communication
9. Development of better leadership
10. Career development and upgrading
11. Improvement in the working environment
12. Improvement in the supervision
13. Better employee feedback to management
14. Participation in educational programs such as seminars, short courses, food shows and exhibitions
15. Giving guest talks at schools and at career days in educational institutions

If employees and their management people wish to learn to work together more effectively, they should determine for themselves what actions, changes, and improvements are desirable and workable. This is in order to achieve the twin and simultaneous goals of the improved quality of work life for all employees of the organization and the greater effectiveness of the organization itself. The causes for ineffectiveness and ways to remedy it are typically within the organization itself.

People want and need to create, to contribute, and to influence their work environment. The work organization provides an opportunity to examine and to experiment with some new behaviors and techniques. Those which prove to be positive are likely to bring about a higher level of organizational effectiveness. The responsibility of the manager is to establish the structures, processes, reward systems and methods that enable each employee to make a larger contribution to the business. But, at the same time, employees will receive more satisfaction from making these contributions. Processes involved in achieving a better quality of work life exist in intelligently practicing good human relations and some applied psychology. These efforts directed at each individual for the purpose of assisting in achieving this improved quality of satisfaction with life as an employee will pay off in greater staff devotion to duty and a more capable foodservice organization.

For further discussion on the quality of work life, see Schuler (1981).

RECOGNITION

One of the easiest ways to build loyalty in the staff is to keep in mind the importance of recognition. A few examples will best illustrate this.

Suppose that the manager receives a very nice compliment about a certain aspect of the foodservice operation. This then should be immediately relayed to the person or persons responsible for the fine performance. So doing results in recognition of the good work that is being done.

Formal recognition can be shown at a dinner in the honor of a person.

Awards of some kind of prize, bonus or plaque can be made. Lapel pins or some other form of overt outward recognition can be issued.

Just a kind word from time to time is an important form of recognition. Saying to a waitress, "my you did a good job with that large dinner party, I am certainly glad we have you on our staff" is a sincere form of recognition that makes the employee feel glad to be a member of the group and that good work is recognized by management.

It is easy to overlook the importance of recognition in a busy day. But the importance of this cannot be overemphasized. Recognition is one of the most significant and psychologically satisfying techniques in the art of management. It should be utilized at every possible opportunity.

TITLES

An important part of a person's job is the title. It is a form of psychic compensation (Townsend 1970). There often is a series of titles—some being lower and some higher and recognized as such in virtually any type of organization.

In the food business, there are some titles that do not appear to be very exciting or imply a minimal amount of prestige. Examples would be a dishwasher, busperson, janitor, pot washer, or vegetable preparer. Using some new imaginative titles that sound better is a good idea. For example, a waiter or waitress in many places is now called a "server"; busperson, a "dining room assistant"; janitor, a "custodian"; a pot washer or dishwasher, a "sanitation engineer or assistant"; a vegetable preparer, a "cook assistant." Other possibilities may occur to you.

Using some imagination in thinking up some attractive titles might do considerable good in raising the prestige level of a particular job and in helping to eliminate recruiting shortages in these various positions. Those people in the organization who aspire to higher levels of responsibility and pay might very well appreciate having a title that indicates as much. An example would be a food preparer who starts as a fry cook, then moves to a sous chef, then chef, then executive chef, then assistant manager for food and beverage and then manager.

SOCIAL INTERCOURSE

It is important that all of the members of your staff be friendly and enjoy one another's company. Developing a feeling like this among the staff is quite effective in increasing morale and productivity.

Parties for the employees held from time to time help to improve morale (See Fig. 1). Everybody should be invited. There might be certain themes for the party. For example, after a highly successful month, a "thanks a million" party could be held. It could be a party with everyone bringing something or a picnic or some other arrangement.

Another idea is to organize sports groups such as a baseball team or bowling team. The uniforms and equipment could be provided by the foodservice at a modest cost. Any type of activity or social event that recognizes the need for employees having a good time together socially away from the job is well worth the cost and effort.

Employee morale must be watched very closely. Any deterioration should be corrected if possible by providing appropriate occasions for enjoying one another's company.

SMOKING

Some states and municipalities have ordinances that require that sections of the dining room be designated for nonsmokers. The foodservice man-

FIG. 1. Summer picnic for employees sponsored by dormitory employer.
Courtesy of Michigan State University Foodservice

agement is more conscious of the problem of smoking if there is such an ordinance than it would be if there were none.

Smoking bothers some people and can even cause an allergic reaction. Also there is concern about unsanitary conditions caused by persons who smoke while cooking food and accidentally drop cigarette ashes into the food.

A section on "smoking" is a requirement of a good policy manual. Whatever the rules may be, they should be clearly stated in a policy manual that each new employee should be required to read. Reasons for having such a smoking policy are sanitation, health, consideration of others and customer preferences. As a rule, customers do not like to see employees smoking on the job.

STRESS

In a work situation, stress occurs when an employee is uncertain as to how to deal with a particular situation. The employee knows that resolving this situation will bring about an important result in his or her life. Stress always involves uncertainty.

An example of a stressful situation is when an applicant is being interviewed for a job. The applicant knows that the success of this interview will have an effect on his or her life.

Stress, of course, is dependent upon the given situation that confronts an individual. What causes stress in one person might not be stressful to another in exactly the same situation.

The reduction of stress or preferably its elimination is a desirable course for management action (Brymer 1982). Stress results in physical ailments and also has a powerful effect on an individual's mental attitude and behavior.

There is a growing concern about stress among employers, and many companies are doing something to manage or reduce stress in their organizations. Alert management is concerned about stress owing to the fact that *worker compensation laws now make an employer legally liable for an employee's mental illness.*

Improving the quality of work life to reduce stress and engaging in other stress-reduction programs involves using human resources more effectively (Brymer 1981). Using job enrichment programs, better work schedules, opening up more opportunities for women and minorities, working on career management plans, educational upgrading and better supervision are all positive procedures.

Supervisors and department heads are the key people in reducing stress. They are the first to detect problems of stress in individual employees. If they can provide counseling and assistance to such persons as soon as such conditions have been observed, a reduction in the amount of stress is likely to occur. Anyone in the organization could suggest ways to reduce stress but the supervisors should be the ones to take the initiative in formulating programs to reduce stress.

Implementation of such programs are most likely to involve job analysis, recruitment, selection, training, development of the individual, career management, wage and salary administration and, if unionized, labor relations.

In summary, perceptive management of employees should preclude any serious problems with stress. However, should such problems arise, prompt and intelligent action to reduce stress will be a very important element in the success of the organization.

Symptoms of Stress

An increased heart rate and frequent headaches are manifestations of stress. For the long term, it may produce ulcers, increased blood pressure and the likelihood of coronary heart disease. For the short term, however, some stress is considered to be beneficial in that it produces additional energies to accomplish wearisome tasks and to cope with difficult situations.

Stress produces irritability and forgetfulness on the part of the individual. Also it may have such negative consequences as absence from the job without permission, low job performance and proneness to accidents.

Dealing with Stress

The way to deal with stress from an individual's standpoint is to learn to be a better manager of time. The organization of one's daily life and the establishment of achievable desirable goals can do much to reduce stress. Sensitivity on the part of management to conditions of stress among employees is a prime requirement for successfully coping with this seemingly growing problem among employees.

Occupational Sources of Stress

Psychologists have identified four causes of employee stress within places of employment. These are (1) the relationship with the immediate supervisor, (2) the rate of pay, (3) the safety conditions in the workplace, and (4) the job security situation (Shostak 1980).

One of the two most commonly identified causes of stress among these four is a boss or supervisor who is constantly after employees to adhere to all of the work rules or even worse to increase production. The rate of pay is the other leading cause of stress. If viewed as unfair, it causes stress, especially if the pay is lower than that of others whom the stressed worker sees as equals. Also, if there are obvious health or safety hazards present in the work areas, stress is a natural reaction. Fear is a major component of stress, and if there is a very obvious lack of safety in the environment, stress results. Another closely related cause of stress is uncertainty about job future. Fear of a layoff is very real to many workers, and they usually want security of employment very badly.

Other conditions on the job also affect the amount of stress. These include the frequency of organizational changes and individual changes and various factors in the physical environment such as temperature, noise, lights, rushing and crowding. Relationships with other workers and the qualities of the job are other stressors. The way the foodservice is structured and the roles that the worker is expected to play can be sources of stress. Lack of career opportunities for some can be stressful.

Recognizing these causes and how they affect individual workers and making an effort to reduce stress are growing areas of responsibility of management today.

THANK YOU

Robert Townsend (1970), the well-known management consultant and author, states that "thanks is a really neglected form of compensation." Now this is indeed true and the manager who wishes to improve employee relations gets off to a quick easy start by simply remembering to say "thank you" every time a situation arises that deserves such acknowledgment. A sincere "thank you" to someone who has just done a favor or who has done an exceptionally good job is one of the best forms of recognition and psychological compensation.

Remember, in the English language, two words that can never be over-worked are "thank you."

UNIONS

Collective bargaining, or organizing, is an effort on the part of employees to band together to act as a single unit when dealing with management over conditions relating to their employment. The union is an authority that negotiates with an employer in behalf of the employees. The usual factors are wages; standard work week; layoffs and firings; hiring and rehiring; scheduling, such as for a guaranteed work week; consecutive days off; overtime provisions; alternative patterns of work, such as part time, short shifts, split shifts, compressed work week; and related considerations. Also included is a provision for the administration of the ensuing agreement, including grievance procedures.

If a foodservice is unionized and an individual takes a job in the company, certain conditions of employment are specified in the formal contract. In these formal agreements there is also a psychological contract, meaning that the employee has certain expectations regarding working conditions, pay, the requirements of the work itself, the amount and nature of the authority of the manager, and probably other considerations.

If an employee becomes dissatisfied with either the formal or psychological aspects of the union contract, this will lead to an attempt to improve the work situation even though there is union representation. There is a strong relationship between the employee's satisfaction with the job and voting for a union. Most employees who vote for a union are dissatisfied while those who are satisfied vote against unionization.

If there is dissatisfaction among some workers, unionization is seldom the first recourse. Usually the first step is an attempt to improve the working situation by an individual employee action alone. An employee who performs some essential job and who is difficult to replace might be able to force the employer to make changes. Or, if an employee who is easy to replace attempts to do this, it is the inclination of management to fire this employee and hire a replacement.

Most workers believe that unions have the power to improve wages and improve working conditions as well as job security and protection for workers. However, other factors of the working situation seem to be coming to the fore at the present time. These are work value changes, meaning that individuals now look to the job for more meaningful work, a sense of achievement, opportunity to grow and possibly a career. Such factors are not enhanced by unionization. Thus, if unionization of employees in the foodservice industry is to grow in the future these factors must be considerations of the union.

A manager can contribute to the level of work dissatisfaction and thus encourage unionization. For example, there can be misleading job interviews so that the new employee's expectations are unrealistic. Or, the job can be so set up that the individual responds poorly to it. Further, the day-to-day management and supervisory control can be so inefficient that the employee feels unfairly treated or unable to communicate with supervisors and managers.

The first step in organizing for a union is a certification election to determine if the majority of the employees want the union. Under American labor law, the union that is certified to represent a group of employees has the sole and exclusive right to bargain for that particular group. Typically, the manager is not very likely to favor the election of a union by the employees. Also, there may be more than one union attempting to win certification as representative of a group of employees.

The stages of the certification process are (1) a campaign to enlist employee support for union representation; (2) the determination of the appropriate union; (3) a preelection campaign by the union and the employers; (4) the election itself; and (5) the certification of the union if the majority voted for the union.

The most essential element in labor–management relations is the bargaining unit. This unit should be truly representative of the workers. After the bargaining unit has been determined, both union and employer embark on a preelection campaign. The union representative will claim to provide a strong voice for the employees emphasizing improvement in wages and working conditions. The employer's emphasis will be on the cost of unionization, the payment of union dues, losses due to strikes and losses of jobs. The NLRB (National Labor Relations Board) conducts the election and certifies the results. If the majority votes for the union, the union will be certified. If the union does not get a majority another election cannot be held for at least a year.

The office of labor–management relations in the U.S. Office of Personnel Management has identified eleven elements essential for effective union–management relations:

1. Acceptance of collective bargaining
2. Balance of power between the union and management
3. Respect for each other's goals
4. Recognition of common goals
5. Well-organized labor relations programs set up by management
6. High level of communication
7. Sincere negotiations
8. Effective administration of the labor contract
9. Comprehensive grievance processes
10. Evaluation by both parties of their relationship
11. Sense of participation in their own welfare on the part of employees (See Biasatti and Martin 1979.)

Deficiencies in these factors are usually associated with increased conflict and a greater number of problems between unions and management (Butler and Caudill 1983).

Grievances

The typical grievance is that conditions of the contract seem to have been violated. A grievance procedure is included in the contract and is used to investigate the problem or condition and to resolve it expeditiously. For example, the filing of a grievance must be done within 7 days of the occasion that is disputed. Usually the grievant reports the violation to union steward and they both go to the supervisor who tries to resolve it at once. If this fails, then the next step is to meet with the assistant manager or general manager. If this fails, the matter (usually) goes to arbitration. The arbitrator must be a person who is acceptable to both worker and the top manager. After a hearing, the arbitrator makes a decision which is binding.

Avoiding Grievances

The number of grievances can be greatly lowered by the manager who follows precisely the rules of the contract. Since most of the grievances involve firings, having a set procedure with plenty of warnings that firing is considered a last resort will do much to reduce such unfortunate incidents. Here are some suggestions:

1. Be certain that all employees know the rules about firings.
2. Be fully informed of all of the facts and circumstances surrounding the case.
3. See that the appropriate union official is also fully informed.
4. Interview the supervisor to be sure you know the reasons for the situation leading up to the decision to dismiss the employee.
5. Review carefully the personnel file of the employee.
6. Make certain that all supervisors are familiar with disciplinary procedures and that they practice these faithfully.

Minimizing or eliminating grievances is good management as such matters are disruptive and demoralizing to the organization. For further discussion, see Chruden and Sherman (1980).

FIRING PEOPLE (AND THOSE WHO QUIT)

The Final Step

The final step in a disciplinary program is firing someone. Typically, warnings are given. For example, two warnings and then the final step is dismissal if the employee persists in violating work rules or other infractions that are detrimental to the organization. There are workers who are capable of effective performance only in certain types of situations. If every effort has been made to find the most suitable situations for a particular employee and all these have failed, then firing is the only alternative.

The Supervisor's Input

However, these situations can be reduced by having each supervisor do a better job of evaluating the performance of their employees (Wasmuth and Davis 1983A–C). A manager should recommend a "thought process" for each supervisor who has an employee who is a candidate for being fired:

The supervisor should be asked to suppose that he/she were before a judge making a statement as to why this employee should be fired. What would be said to the judge? If the judge asks, "How many times has the employee been told that he/she was doing a poor job and what to do to improve performance?" could this be answered adequately? If the judge asked, "How long has this employee been doing an unsatisfactory job?" could this be answered? Also, could the supervisor answer: "Why was this condition allowed to exist for so long?"

The purpose of the preceding dialogue is to bring to the attention of managers and supervisors that this is not a one-sided situation. Sometimes the firing was brought about by a series of mismanagement moves that deprived the employee of the proper supervision and that might have been avoided had this unfortunate situation been investigated sooner and corrective action taken. Good management, thus, indicates that probably both the employee and the supervisor were at fault if the employee has to be fired. The "contribution" of the supervisor will help minimize the number of people who have to be fired and also build a reputation among the other employees that people who get fired certainly deserve to be. Their firing was strictly based upon their failure to perform under the most favorable and competent supervision.

Firing should not be postponed, once the decision has been made. The employee should be fired on the spot, given the pay that has been earned, and told to leave promptly. The manager or supervisor should not be exposed to any questioning from the employee nor request information from the employee being fired. Details should not be related to others.

Exit Interviews

An exit interview is recommended when an employee quits. The manager will find out facts about this person's employment that cannot be determined in any other way. Employees never see the organization in the same way as the manager or supervisor. Thus, factors in their employment might be brought forth that will be of considerable value in helping avoid any future firings or resignations. A departing employee is free to say whatever he or she wishes. Such candid descriptions of the conditions that brought about the employee's departure often can provide valuable information useful for improving employee management in the future.

REFERENCES

BIASATTI, L.L. and MARTIN, J.E. 1979. A measure of the quality of union–management relations. J. Appl. Psych. *64*, 387–390.

BRYMER, R.A. 1981. Stress management for management stress. The Cornell Hotel and Restaurant Administration Quarterly *20*, 61–69.

BRYMER, R.A. 1982. Stress and your employees. The Cornell Hotel and Restaurant Administration Quarterly *22*, 61–66.

BUTLER, R.L. and CAUDILL, D.S. 1983. Bargaining for broke: The need to negotiate cutbacks. The Cornell Hotel and Restaurant Administration Quarterly *24*, 43–47.

CHRUDEN, H.J. and SHERMAN, A.W. 1980. Personnel Management: The Utilization of Human Resources. South-Western Publishing Co., Cincinnati, OH.

NEBEL, E.C. 1978. Motivation, leadership, and employee performance: A review. The Cornell Hotel and Restaurant Administration Quarterly *19*, 62–69.

SARGENT, A.G. 1981. The Androgynous Manager, Amacom, New York, NY.

SCHULER, R.S. 1981. Personnel and Human Relations Management. West Publishing Co., St. Paul, MN.

SHOSTAK, A.B. 1980. Blue-Collar Stress. Addison-Wesley Publishing Co., Reading, MA.

TOWNSEND, R. 1970. Up the Organization. Alfred A. Knopf. New York, NY.

WASMUTH, W.J. and DAVIS, S.W. 1983A. Managing employee turnover. The Cornell Hotel and Restaurant Administration Quarterly *23*, 15–22.

WASMUTH, W.J. and DAVIS, S.W. 1983B. Managing employee turnover: Why employees leave. The Cornell Hotel and Restaurant Administration Quarterly *24*, 11–18.

WASMUTH, W.J. and DAVIS, S.W. 1983C. Strategies for managing employee turnover. The Cornell Hotel and Restaurant Administration Quarterly *24*, 65–75.

Developing Communication Skills

BEING UNDERSTOOD

Communication is the process of passing information from one person to another. The ability to do this and practicing it are surely keys to success. It is one thing to know something and want to communicate it. But, it is an altogether different matter to successfully communicate the information so that the other person fully understands the message. How is this best done?

Step 1. First it is necessary to fully appreciate the importance of communication and of being understood (Stoner 1982). Being a poor communicator is probably the most common weakness in managers. They know what they want and what they expect of employees—but they fail to adequately inform those who must understand the thoughts of the manager. On the average, supervisors and department heads spend about 80% of their working time giving and receiving communications. So, this ability *is* very important. If communication is poor, the results will be misunderstandings, inefficiency, waste, high blood pressure, poor morale, bad feelings, and confusion.

Step 2. Improving communication means recognizing that it is definitely a two-way process. There must be a sender and a receiver to have communication. Unless the information has been received and understood by the receiver, communication has not taken place. Many managers make the mistake of assuming that because they have issued some kind of message, that communication has taken place. Not necessarily so!

Step 3.   It is important to realize that for good communication, one must decide on the reason or goal of the communication and the specific words and information to be used before deciding on what medium to be used to transmit the message. For example, an ineffective message could go hastily out in the form of a bulletin board notice. But most likely the words chosen and the desired outcome were not very well thought out.

Step 4.   One must know the types or channels of communication. The most common channel is from the general manager to the subordinate managers or supervisors. Then, they communicate to those people who are concerned, in their departments. This first type is called *downward* communication. The second type is *upward* communication, which goes in just the opposite direction. This type is just as important as the downward type. Employees should be trained and encouraged to keep their supervisors and managers informed. Middle managers are the links between the line employees and the general manager. An easy and free communication link between all members of the business organization is essential for good management. Anything less will mean a loss of productivity and morale. Managers must impress on all employees that they want to hear the truth and they want the information as soon as it is feasible to obtain it. The third type is *horizontal* communication. This occurs among employees in the same department or between managers of different departments. Like the other types, this is also an essential part of management and must be encouraged in every possible way.

Step 5.   A policy of encouraging as much communication as is needed for the best operation of the business is recommended. Staff must realize that before any communication is attempted, the message should be thought through so that it is now clear and firm. Unless this is done first, a communicator cannot presume that the message is going to be fully understood. The communicator should mentally consider, "What is to be said and what should be achieved as a result of this communication?"

Step 6.   It is important to decide on the means by which the communication is to be transmitted. Usually it is spoken or written, but it could be conveyed in other ways, such as by pictures or symbols. Even "body language" conveys a great deal, as does personal appearance and gestures. Movements of the hands, shoulders, head, and facial expressions tell a lot. Generally, spoken words are the best means to communicate because if the listener does not understand (and always feels free to ask questions), the listener will ask to have the statement repeated to make it clearer. This makes it a two-way communication and that is the best. If the communication is in writing, the writer cannot be very sure that the reader understood. (Are you understanding this?!) Written communications are needed, however, under certain circumstances. When writing, it is necessary to use words that are easily understood.

Step 7. One must recognize the main barriers to good communication. These are inborn in people and should be considered when planning any messages. Some people just do not want to hear or learn. They see no need to have this particular message. Others have such fear of the "boss" that they hardly hear what was said. These same limitations apply to upward communication also. Some employees like the way they do things and do not want to change anything. So, they do not pay much attention to the message. Using very understandable language and making sure the receiver understood by some kind of feedback system are good procedures. Looking at the face of the receiver when giving the message is usually the best method of determining whether the message was understood or not. If the listener looks a little puzzled, it is better to repeat it. Unless the listener feels talked down to, repeating messages is also good, as a little repetition often helps.

Actions speak louder than words, so if a message is supposed to produce certain results, then the managers could show the desired outcomes. The manager should never violate some rule that his/her subordinates are expected to honor.

Step 8. The last step is the recognition of the informal information system called the "grapevine." When employees spread rumors and pass information along, it is very likely to be inaccurate (Morgan 1981). Sometimes a manager can obtain useful insights into the morale of the staff by listening to some of the grapevine gossip. When the leaders who spread rumors are known, they should be kept from spreading falsehoods that could do harm. If such false information is being passed around, then the supervisor or manager must immediately discredit such information by providing the facts and truth. Rumors can be minimized by the elimination of uncertainties and fears among the employees. An "open door" policy and free movement of persons and information throughout the entire organization can do much to reduce, but probably not eliminate, rumors and scuttlebutt. If the management team really tries to keep all of their people fully informed and they do so promptly by communicating the facts, this positive, accurate information will largely replace the usually inaccurate rumors. Doing so is a positive, intelligent counter to the grapevine. And it is also very good management.

LISTENING

One of the easiest and most effective ways for a manager to improve ability is to be a better communicator. And, among these methods is being a better listener. The University of Minnesota has determined that immediately after someone has listened to another person talk, he or she remem-

FIG. 1. Clear, understandable communication is a
key supervisory ability.
*Courtesy of Michigan State
University Foodservice*

bers only about half of what was heard—no matter how carefully the listener
thought they were listening. Then, as time passes, say 2 months after
listening to a talk, the average listener will remember only about 25% of
what was said. In fact, after having just learned something, a person can
forget from one-third to one-half of it within 8 hours. One forgets more in
this short interval than one does in the next 6 months. One of the main uses
of time in a manager's day is devoted to listening; see Fig. 1. In fact,
executives state that as much as 80% of their time is spent listening to
someone. Or, they spend much time having someone listening to them.

Ways for Improvement

To improve listening ability, two things are necessary: (1) creating awareness of the factors that affect listening ability and (2) building the type of
aural (listening) experience that can produce good listening habits.

The basic problem is that we think much faster than we talk. We speak
about 125 words per minute. The brain of an average person contains about
13 billion brain cells and operates in a very complicated but efficient
fashion—much faster than our speaking apparatus can produce words. To

improve listening ability, one should try to reduce the speed of one's thinking. Because words play such a large part of the thinking process, it is important to try to train one's brain to receive words at a pace that is extremely slow compared with the speed of the brain in absorbing these words. In trying to slow down the brain during the listening process, the brain tends to mix up the words to which one is listening with other thoughts that are in the brain at the same time. The result is that the thoughts that are assembled because of this mixture are different than the words that were actually spoken. The problem is that one can listen and still have spare time for thinking. One adds thoughts, in terms of words, to those being communicated. The resulting mixture is not a true interpretation of what was being told. This condition complies with the first requirement—that one builds awareness of the factors affecting listening ability. In other words, one must be aware that his/her brain mixes its words with the words that come from the partner in conversation. Consequently one must slow down the thinking process and not complicate the conversation with personal thoughts. This means trying to concentrate on what the person is saying and eliminating thoughts that have a tendency to mix words with those thoughts being delivered in conversation.

How does one build the experiences that produce good listening habits? It is necessary to direct the maximum amount of thought to the message being received, leaving a minimum amount of time for mental excursions on sidetracks that lead away from the talker's thoughts. Here are some suggestions:

1. Try to think ahead of the person who is talking, anticipating what the conversation is leading to and what conclusions may be drawn from the words being spoken, at that particular moment.

2. Weigh each word used by the talker to support the points that that talker is trying to make to you. This means asking the question, "Is this evidence really valid?" Or, "Is this evidence quite complete?"

3. Periodically review and mentally summarize the principal points of the conversation that have been completed thus far.

4. Review thoughts that may not have been put into actual words. For example, pay attention to nonverbal communications such as gestures, facial expressions, tone of voice, and body movements and see if they add meaning to the spoken word. Ask the question, "Is the person talking to me trying to avoid some subject or beating around the bush?"

Try to Listen for Ideas

An idea is something that is built in the mind of one person and hopefully precisely rebuilt in the mind of the person to whom the communication is directed. The person speaking takes the thought apart and puts the thought in terms of a group of words. The receiver mentally reassembles the thought as it was understood. As a receiver, one must know what to listen for in order to reconstruct accurately the thought that has been transmitted. If there are parts of the thought that are not clear, it is important to ask questions in order to complete in one's own mind the reassembly of the thought which was originally in the mind of the speaker.

Warning about Emotions

One of the main hindrances to good listening is the tendency to mentally turn off what one does not want to hear. On the other hand, all ears are open to that which one wants to hear whether it is the truth or pure bunk. When listening to something that one wishes not to hear, there is a tendency to plan a rebuttal and flatly turn down the thoughts of the speaker. So doing reinforces one's own thoughts that support personal feelings on the subject.

For example, suppose that the chef suggests to his manager that they buy a certain make and type of kitchen equipment. Sometime in the past another kind of equipment was purchased from this same company that makes the equipment that the chef wants, and this purchase turned out to be a disaster. Consequently the manager's thought processes immediately turn off the idea. The new product which the chef suggests may be a vast improvement over any machines that the company has manufactured in the past. It may be a superb piece of equipment for the kitchen. Any conversation with a mental or emotional outburst that the products of this particular company are "no good" is based upon an emotional rather than a rational consideration of the chef's request.

Upward Listening

Given a sufficient number of avenues for movement of information upward, there is no reason why better listening cannot be achieved. An example of this is a worker who wishes to talk to his/her supervisor. The supervisor then talks to the general manager. How effectively does this work? All evidence indicates that the degree of success of an organization depends on how well and how easily this process functions. Some of the very best ideas occur to those on the working line. These people are intimately aware of the problem and have some ideas as to how it may be solved. Thus, efforts on the part of all managers to improve listening ability will pay off in a better, more productive, and profitable operation.

MEETINGS

Meetings are essential for good management. There must be communication and some types of communication are best done in a meeting; see Fig. 2. The manager should meet with supervisors and department heads once each week (Townsend 1970). The meeting should probably be on the same day at the same time so that the habit of attendance becomes part of the routine of the organization. An agenda for the meeting should be communicated to each supervisor in advance. Methods for doing this vary but the easiest and simplest method is to post the agenda on the bulletin board at least 2 or 3 days in advance. Each supervisor is responsible for reviewing the notice that is posted at a regular time each week. So doing gives each person who is going to attend the meeting an opportunity to think about the subjects that will be discussed and to come up with some ideas to contribute. Not to do this means that each person who comes to the meeting approaches the problem "cold" with insufficient time to give adequate thought to the topic(s) being discussed.

There must be a reason for the meeting and a need to bring people together. If there are no problems that need discussion, then the meeting should be cancelled. But this may not occur very often in most organizations because of the changing and complex situations that seem to be the rule these days. Meetings should be kept short. For a *really short meeting*, there

FIG. 2. Dining room staff hears manager explain new procedures. Such meetings, when needed, are an excellent method of communication.

should be no chairs at all in the room. It is essential to start on time and end on time.

A summary of the accomplishments of the meeting should be distributed to each participant. It could be posted on the bulletin board or communicated in some other way. So doing will provide a reminder of what was achieved at the meeting. The use of visual aids at meetings is highly recommended as people will remember what they see and hear much longer and better than by oral communication alone.

Meetings also provide two-way communication in the group. This is a valuable attribute of holding regular meetings. However, verbose groups or individuals should not be allowed to monopolize the time. Use of parliamentary procedures is advisable.

ORGANIZATION CHARTS AND ORGANIZATION

Benefits of Good Organization

1.   Each person knows what the jobs are to be performed.
2.   Assignments are definite.
3.   Each employee can concentrate on fullfilling his or her particular mission in an efficient manner.
4.   There is a minimum of misunderstanding and confusion.
5.   Each employee knows *who* should do *what*.
6.   Each employee knows his/her supervisor.
7.   Each employee knows who is over or under him/her. Consequently, each person knows to whom to go down to for getting a particular job done and done well. Likewise, the person knows to whom to go up to for advice or information or assistance.
8.   The authority necessary to accomplish the job is delegated according to how best the work can be accomplished. This makes possible the effective production of work.
9.   Good organization maximizes resource utilization and productive results.

How to Organize a Foodservice

1.   Know the objectives of the overall organization and that of each department or section.
2.   Break the work to be done down into its component activities.

3. Group the activities into practical units.

4. For each activity or practical unit, define clearly the duties to be carried out.

5. Provide the physical working environment, tools, equipment, supplies, pictures, or other aids that are necessary for each practical unit.

6. Assign qualified personnel according to the needs of each unit.

7. Delegate the required authority and responsibility to the assigned personnel.

Organization Charts

Some advantages in preparing an organization chart are as follows:

1. The person who prepares the chart benefits from the thinking needed to set the chart up in the first place. In other words, preparing a chart requires a study of the structure of the organization.

2. Overlapping operations can be corrected or modified.

3. Duplications can be eliminated.

4. Authoritative sources of information for all employees can be established.

5. Official answers can be found.

6. The charts support the achievement of goals.

However, these tools cannot include everything affecting the organization structure owing to the informal lines of communication and informal relationships pertaining to members of the organization. There will always be informal lines of communication and information that is not shown on the organization chart.

Another version of an organization chart is known as an *activity chart*. The activity chart shows each employee's job or activity. These activities may be illustrated in the form of diagrams or pictures, and the relationship between each of the units is illustrated in the form of diagrams and a chart. Some organization charts show their customers at the top of the chart and the manager at the bottom. Such an unusual arrangement impresses on the employees the importance of the customer. Also, it illustrates that the manager who is shown at the bottom of the chart has as a foremost responsibility the support of all the employees, shown above him/her, who are serving the customer.

Figure 3 illustrates a type of organization chart that emphasizes the team approach. The goals of the business dominate the conceptualization of the chart.

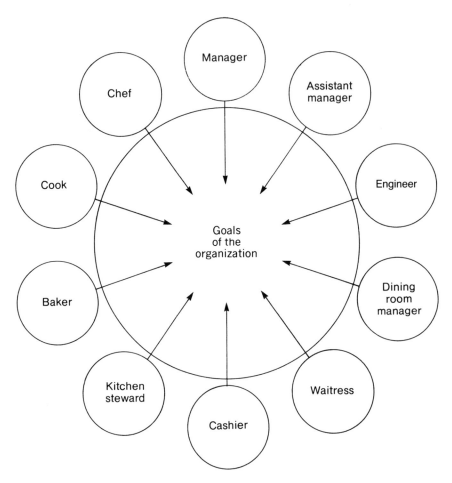

FIG. 3. Organization chart—team approach. *Comments*: Each person on the staff is dedicated to the achievement of the organization's goals. Instead of emphasizing hierarchical relationships this type of chart pictorializes the mutual relationships of everyone employed in the foodservice towards the organization's success.

POLICY MANUALS

It is highly recommended that a policy manual be used. This manual sets forth all of the basic policies and rules of the organization. Each new employee must read the manual. After reading the manual, the employee signs a statement that is then torn out from the manual and placed in the employee's file. So doing proves that the employee has read the manual and certifies that he/she understands the contents of the manual. The employee keeps his/her copy of the manual for future reference.

Contents of the manual often include a brief history of the company and the basic philosophies of service and quality of product to which the company adheres. The manual can include details about such things as the system of discipline, noting that it includes a verbal warning system, written warnings, and then final dismissal if the employee does not stay within the policies of the company. Other items often included in the manual are as follows: the dress code, smoking restrictions, pay policies, tips, holidays, maternity leave, suggestion awards, meals, vacations, insurance and other compensations. All of this is essential information about which an employee should be fully aware.

Table of Contents

The table of contents of a policy manual might look something like the following:

1. About your new employer
2. Your pay and other benefits:

   • Pay scales
   • Pay reviews
   • Tips
   • Paydays
   • Insurance protection
   • Deductions made from your pay
   • Meals while working
   • Vacations and holidays
   • Absences from work
   • Maternity provisions
   • Educational assistance
   • Awards for suggestions
   • Incentive programs

3. While you are working:

   • Your training program
   • Grooming and appearance
   • Punctuality and reliability
   • Smoking
   • Code of discipline, rules and penalties
   • Job problems

4. Career opportunities:

   • Job assignments and changes
   • Promotion policies

Procedural manual.   More information is given by an instructional or procedural type of manual that explains a particular job or duty. Such a manual describes step by step how a particular function is to be performed. An example might be that of a bus person. Bussing should be done immediately after the table is cleared and there is a certain method by which the bussing must be done. The step sequence can be outlined in a procedural manual. In fact, after a bus person is hired and trained, it might be advisable to give this person an examination in written form to be sure that the person understands the necessary steps to comply with the procedures relating to bussing tables. The same concept can be used in any other portion of the foodservice operation. Another example of this would be the use of pictures for a cook as to how a particular standard dish should look when it is completed and ready to serve to the customer.

TOURING THE PREMISES

Providing a tour of the premises for the new employee gives an opportunity to explain where coats are to be hung, where lockers are provided, where the various departments are located and what they look like, where to park, what door to use, and other similar matters. The new employee can be introduced to the various department heads and to the person under which he/she will be working. Such a system of new employee orientation does much to convince this employee of the thoroughness and care that the organization exhibits towards its workers. Such a favorable first impression convinces the employee that this foodservice must be well managed and a very good place to work.

REFERENCES

MORGAN, W.J. 1981. Supervision and Management of Quantity Food Preparation, 2nd Edition. McCutchan Publishing Corp., Berkeley, CA.
STONER, J.A.F. 1982. Management, 2nd Edition. Prentice-Hall, Inc., Englewood Cliffs, NJ.
TOWNSEND, R. 1970. Up the Organization. Alfred A. Knopf, New York, NY.

BIBLIOGRAPHY

WHYTE, W.F. (A classic study.) (Reprint.) Communications in the food-service industry. The Cornell Hotel and Restaurant Administration Quarterly, Ithaca, NY.

Increasing Productivity

PAYROLL PRODUCTIVITY

Improving productivity is one of the most important goals of foodservice managers today. So doing is absolutely essential to staying competitive and remaining profitable in the future.

Targets

The following are targets for improving productivity:

- Sales volume
- Food and beverage quality
- Service
- Advertising and other sales support effectiveness
- Specific food and beverage production jobs, goals and standards

The following are *not* direct targets of productivity improvement:

- Employee safety
- Employee relations
- Training programs
- Employee compensation procedures
- Labor expense control

Definition

Productivity could be defined as a function of how much food and beverage can be produced in 1 hour of paid work (Freshwater and Bragg 1975). Increasing productivity helps to offset rising labor costs and rising menu prices.

Another definition of productivity might be output compared to input. One can define *output* as the total gross sales or covers (number of persons served) or similar measure best suited to the particular operation. *Input* can be defined as the total of major costs of producing the output.

Productivity might be thought of as the overall efficiency of the food-service—dollar volume compared to major cost items. For example, productivity can be defined as the difference between sales and the total of labor costs and food−beverage costs. Thus, the higher the sales and the lower the sum of these major costs, the higher the productivity.

But any consideration of productivity relates right back to the productivity of each individual employee (Lane 1976).

Steps for Managerial Improvement

You must first improve *managerial* productivity in order to increase *employee* productivity. Each manager must have a very clear concept of what improving productivity is all about. Without this, no manager can explain these concepts to staff.

The next step is to vigorously strengthen management awareness, knowledge, skills and perceptions so that each manager can become the planner and doer of productivity improvements.

The third step is to focus on middle management people such as supervisors and department heads. Sometimes there is actually a conflict between incentive systems and motivation to work at the peak of effectiveness. Such a condition should be carefully evaluated to determine if such conflicts exist. Good middle management people are looking for more interesting and vital work. They welcome a chance to find new commitments which they deem worthy of their talents and skills. Thus, projects to increase productivity within their realm will be seen as a welcome challenge.

Job Satisfaction vs. Productivity

There is a clear difference between job satisfaction and motivation to work hard or productivity. Employees can be very satisfied because their particular jobs are easy. Conversely, they can be dissatisfied because they want to do a good job and their organization is putting obstacles in the way of their doing an outstanding job.

Foodservice owners and managers want to create job satisfactions that come from a strong positive motivation. They cannot use measures of job satisfaction to tell about success in motivation and job effectiveness productivity.

Improving Job Productivity

Such improvement can be achieved in six ways:

1. Set high standards for productivity improvement.

2. Try to be as flexible as possible in responding to customer needs and wants in products and services.

3. Make sure all products and services are of excellent quality and performed in a timely manner.

4. Select and develop skilled, motivated and enthusiastic managers who are dedicated to their jobs and careers and want to learn more about productivity and growth for themselves and their staffs.

5. Create a genuine atmosphere for true teamwork.

6. Recognize and reward outstanding performance of any and all employees, regardless of position or job.

Implementing Productivity Improvement

To implement a productivity improvement program, an initial diagnosis should be made to see where improvements are needed. All manager and staff members should be interviewed to find out where they feel they could improve their own productivity. Each manager must be willing and able to do his/her share. But, remember, full support is necessary from the general manager from the very outset.

It is necessary to *start small* and be reasonably sure the plan will work. One must be sure to employ the best possible ideas, methods, measurements and feedback for this first trial project. If it proves to be successful, then one should move on to other and bigger things. Managers must be placed in the cutting edge of these efforts. They should be responsible for shaping the details of the productivity project of their employees. Then the owner or general manager measures the successes achieved and can reward the managers for increases in productivity in their departments.

If even 1 hour of nonproductive work each day could be turned into productive work, substantial improvements would result. Is not the effort worthwhile?

STAFF PLANNING AND SCHEDULING

One of the most effective ways to increase productivity and efficiency is to engage in more meaningful staff planning and expert employee scheduling. This is the process whereby personnel requirements for a given period are predetermined with reference to the work units expected to be performed. The advantages of staff planning are as follows:

1. Distributing staff according to the expected work load
2. Measuring effectiveness of supervisors in scheduling their people
3. Ascertaining current labor costs
4. Identifying changes in labor costs in relation to sales or value of production

The essential elements of good staff planning are as follows:

1. Setting standards for productivity
2. Doing forecasting
3. Establishing a scale of staffing requirements
4. Determining the weekly work schedules
5. Making the daily or weekly labor reports
6. Producing the weekly productivity reports

Setting Standards of Productivity

Step 1. Determine present productivity.   What is the labor cost trend? What are present payroll costs and work schedules? How do labor costs relate to the sales or product value? If unionized, one must consider any restraints on scheduling that may be in the contract. It will be necessary to work around these constraints. One should make a trend analysis over the past year to see what is happening; especially important is the ratio of payroll costs to sales (payroll costs divided by sales or the value of production). These ratios can be computed by weeks or months, but weekly is preferred for better control. Doing this may reveal weaknesses which then command attention if productivity is to be improved.

Step 2. Compute an hourly volume count.   This could be in terms of covers (number of people) served or sales volume. A similar count could be made for the bar. Counts are made each hour that the foodservice is open for business.

Step 3. Determine what productivity has been in the past by using two charts—employee work schedules and historic volume counts.   See Figs. 1 and 2. An analysis of these includes computation of work units per man/woman hour. (Hereinafter, reference will be to "man hour" for convenience.) This figure is calculated by dividing total work units (covers served or

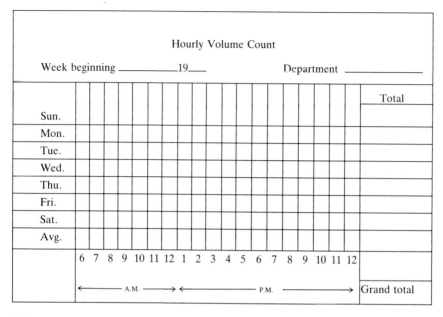

FIG. 1. Hourly customer count record. *Comments*: This chart summarizes the historic volume count of customers. Obtaining such statistics is part of step 3 to determine employee work productivity that has occurred in the past.

sales volume) per week by the total man hours for that week. This will give the average work units or sales per man hour. Average work units per man day are found by multiplying average work units per man hour by the average number of hours worked by employees in a day. For average work units per man week, multiply man-day productivity by the number of work days in a week. These computations thus produce historic productivity standards.

Step 4.   Make a judgment as to the desirable productivity goal.   Considerations should be as follows:

- Size and physical layout of the foodservice
- Nature of the operation, i.e., hospital, dormitory, restaurant, club, or others
- Type of menu
- Location
- Level of customer or guest service desired

Once the standards have been tentatively decided upon, they should be discussed with the subordinate managers to arrive at a consensus of the desired productivity goals.

Weekly Employee Schedule										
Week beginning _____ 19___					Department _____					
Employee's names	Position	Pay rate	Sun.	Mon.	Tue.	Wed.	Thu.	Fri.	Sat.	Total hours

Grand total hours _____

FIG. 2. Employee work schedule record. *Comments*: Purpose of using this chart is to summarize hours worked in 1 week by staff. Compiling this is part of step 3 to determine what employee work productivity has been in the past. The other exercise is use of Fig. 1 to determine historic customer volume counts.

Doing Forecasting

To do forecasting one should get the help of assistant managers and probably involve department heads and selected employees. In making the forecast, one must consider such factors as any previous forecasts made for a comparable period vs. the actual results that have been experienced. Under consideration also should be such factors as group reservations, special events, conventions in the city, athletic contests, seasonal or weather factors and any other influence that might affect business. The period for the forecast can vary, although 10 days seems like a good choice. There could be 3 overlapping days for making minor adjustments. In making the estimates, one must forecast the number of food covers (number of persons served) and the dollar volume of sales or product value. The same should be done for the bar. Then it is necessary to schedule the optimum staff needed to adequately serve this demand.

One must always compare actual results with forecasts. So doing sharpens the ability to make forecasts. One should not be discouraged by wide misses. Forecasts will continually become better as experience is gained in making them. For each forecast, it is helpful to make a percentage of error calculation—and these should gradually become smaller!

The results of all this should be a slow-but-steady improvement in the scheduling of staff to match expected volume of business. Increases in productivity and profits should be the happy result.

Establishing a Scale of Staffing Requirements

A tabulation is now made of the staffing requirements for the various levels of business that have been forecasted. For example, the hourly productivity standard might be 1 waitress for each 15 covers; 1 bus person per 75 covers; and 1 cook per 60 covers. Another important consideration is to determine the minimum staff requirements at any given time. These people provide the necessary minimum services to stay open. The maximum staff must also be fixed when a full house load is expected. Thus, there is a range of employees needed at any particular time. This number is based on minimum, maximum and proportional changes in staff needs based upon the anticipated levels of business.

Determining Weekly Work Schedules

An optimum weekly scheduling level for any type of position can be made based upon the standard that seems to be the correct one (Freshwater and Bragg 1975).

Suppose the foodservice is forecasting 200 customers on the average per day for the coming 10 days. However, on Friday, 250 are expected. First, one should make an approximate count of the daily distribution of customers on sample days. Suppose 35% of the customers come for breakfast, 45% for lunch and 20% for dinner. If the hourly standard for waitresses is 15 covers per waitress, there should be 4 waitresses scheduled for breakfast (200 × 35% = 70 customers ÷ 15 = 4.6 = 4 waitresses). Four should be able to handle the breakfast load. For lunch, one should schedule 6 waitresses (200 × 45% = 90 customers ÷ 15 = 6 waitresses). For dinner one should schedule 3 servers (200 × 20% = 40 ÷ 15 = 2.6 or 3 waitresses). As dinner requires more service, 3 servers should be scheduled. For Friday, one should schedule 6 servers for breakfast (250 × 35% = 90 customers ÷ 15 = 6 waitresses). For lunch one needs to schedule 8 service people (250 × 45% = 113 customers ÷ 15 = 7.5 servers) and for dinner one should schedule 7 waitresses (250 × 40% = 100 customers ÷ 15 = 6.6 or 7 waitresses).

During periods of slow business, the staff would be reduced to a minimum or appropriate level. During peak periods, the use of short-shift people who arrive at the most needed times is the most productive scheduling strategy. Knowing the pattern of patronage is thus essential.

If the foodservice operates 7 days a week, the 5-day-week people must be replaced for 2 days. As for which 2 days an employee will have off—this is the prerogative of management. However, the employee's preference should be considered and accommodated to the extent possible.

Here is an opportunity for the use of alternative work arrangements, particularly differentiated staffing—the use of a permanent skeletal staff aided by part-time employees. Part-time people are readily available in most locations, thus this should be a very satisfactory arrangement.

Also helpful is having full-time staff members who are fully capable of performing in more than one job. Such flexibility aids productivity especially on certain days when other regular staff are off duty. Extra pay may be needed for employees who perform certain jobs when being rotated, but even so, the use of employees on more than one job is very advantageous. The extra cost of training such people for alternative jobs is well worth it. This policy greatly eases the problem of scheduling days off, providing substitutes during vacation periods, and is often vital for covering emergencies and unexpected demands. If unionized, there may be requirements for higher pay scales for certain job-rotated positions.

Making the Daily or Weekly Labor Report

Statistics on the total hours of staff work in the various departments is a helpful control device. Summaries are made of the total hours worked at regular pay rates, the number of overtime hours worked, and hours of part-time work. The totals for each department are then extended. A grand total of all hourly staff is then compiled. This total is then related to the number of covers served or customer count in order to evaluate the labor productivity for this particular period.

Producing the Weekly Productivity Report

This report summarizes the labor productivity based upon the daily or weekly labor report. Then the total labor hours and the labor costs are compared to the total sales or value of production for the same period.

These actual figures are also compared to the estimates made during the forecasting exercise to see how accurate they turned out to be. So doing gives an excellent appraisal of the labor productivity as well as the accuracy of the forecasting.

Producing the productivity report over time brings about refinements in the methods of reporting and a higher degree of forecasting accuracy. Constant effort can then be devoted to adjusting the staffing to optimum levels in order to maximize labor productivity.

ALTERNATIVE WORK PROVISIONS

One way to increase productivity is to build a work scheduling and hiring system that fully utilizes the talents of all of the employees. There are three main variations on this theme (Schuler 1981).

1. Options that rearrange daily work schedules:

   a. *Flextime* in which employees have some choice over daily hours but usually requires an 8-hour day and a 40-hour work week.
   b. *Compressed work week* wherein a 35- or 40-hour work week is compressed by longer daily hours into less than 5 days per week or less than 10 days in 2 weeks.

2. Options involving paid or unpaid leave time:

   a. *Voluntary leave* which is time off from work for a specific period, usually without pay, but with a clear understanding of reinstatement in the job upon termination of the leave.
   b. *Sabbatical leave* intended to allow the recipient free time to pursue educational endeavors, usually with partial pay and/or benefits.
   c. *Personal service leave* to work for VISTA, Peace Corps, or some similar public service job for a specified period of time.

3. Options providing employees with less than full-time jobs:

   a. *Work sharing* is the reduction in hours worked due to a turndown in business. It is an alternative to a layoff. The employee has no choice in this option.
   b. *Part-time employment* is simply hiring people on a regular basis for less than the usual work week hours.
   c. *Differentiated staffing* is the use of a permanent full-time skeletal staff aided by part-time employees.
   d. *Job sharing* means that two people perform the work and responsibilities of one full-time position. Each person's pay and fringe benefits are prorated according to the division of work time.

e. *Job splitting* is essentially the same as job sharing except that each of the two employees assume a specific responsibility for a clearly defined portion of what was once a full-time job.

Rearranging Daily Work Schedules

Flextime is the most popular nonstandard work schedule (Schuler 1981). Use of this arrangement is suitable to the (usually) long hours of daily operation. It tends to decrease absenteeism, increase employee morale, encourage a higher level of employee participation in decision making, and usually leads to better labor–management relations. Personal preferences, travel problems in getting to work, and increasing desire for more discretion on the part of both management and employees tend to favor this arrangement. It does somewhat complicate scheduling tasks of supervisors, however.

Compressed work weeks are appealing to some workers who highly value greater freedom for personal pursuits such as education. This arrangement tends to decrease turnover and absenteeism. It can also be used for employees who just want to work on weekends and put in, for example, two 12-hour days, or two other days to replace 5-day workers.

Options for Paid or Unpaid Leave Time

The perceptive manager will recognize the occasional need for this type of leave, particularly for those yearning for more education. Military reservists would be another example. Reassurance that the job will be there at the end of the leave is the predominant stipulation.

Providing Permanent Part-Time Work and Job Sharing

Differentiated staffing can take several forms, but it is quite suitable for foodservices. The skeletal job coverage is provided by full-time workers and supplemented by part-time or permanent part-time employees. McDonald's Corporation utilizes this arrangement.

Job sharing or splitting is really quite different than part-time employment. The main difference is that the two people who share the job work together as a team, and thus they must frequently communicate and coordinate their work activities.

Experience has shown that such workers tend to be very motivated and professional in their attitude. Thus, they are likely to be productive and dedicated workers. Each job sharer divides the pay and the benefits of that particular job. This seems to make each one feel that he/she is an integral part of the foodservices working team. Such feelings strengthen their affiliation, their loyalty to the organization and their morale.

Employing job sharers is likely to reduce costs because experience indicates that the sharers will be more prompt, use less sick leave, and be absent less than other employees. If one sharer becomes ill, the other can temporarily fill in, thus continuing the job that otherwise would have been vacant or absorbed as extra work by the remaining staff.

Shorter work hours seem to result in high energy levels and more enthusiasm. Supervisors report that job sharers do more than their 50% and accomplish more, proportionately. There is more job satisfaction, less stress, less boredom and less conflict with other workers. There are also fewer conflicts with family responsibilities.

Sometimes a full-time worker considers quitting due to nonjob commitments. By utilizing job sharing and establishing a reduced working schedule, this valuable employee can be retained on the job.

In other instances, a very competent person might be available but only as a job sharer. This arrangement provides the advantages of using this person's ability and at the same time providing a productive outlet for a talented individual.

Groups That Favor Job Sharing

This work option is appealing to many women who contemplate a full-time job with uneasiness. Family and home responsibilities create mental frictions. Job sharing provides an opportunity to utilize their talents. Such arrangements have a further national benefit in more adequate care of children and better mental health of conflicted parents.

Those approaching retirement age are often seeking reduced work loads but wish to continue to contribute their knowledge and skills to their employing organization. Job sharing or part-time work gives them an outlet for their talents and, at the same time, a reduced work load which frees up time for the enjoyment of personal ventures (Cohen and Gadon 1978).

Teenagers have many outside interests with school and other activities. Job sharing is a very appealing work arrangement in this age group.

Possible Disadvantages of Job Sharing

Employers may wonder who wants to work at such reduced hours? The answer is believed to be a rather low proportion (under 10%) of the total work force. But, as noted above, there are many who are interested.

Would training costs rise? Yes, they might, but if turnover can be reduced, which is likely, the net cost is going to be less.

Administrative costs would probably be slightly higher due to somewhat more paper work.

The cost of fringe benefits should not be any higher than for a full-time job holder. This would not be true if the basis for the cost is the number of employees rather than wages paid or hours worked.

An example of a same cost situation would be providing a 2-week paid vacation for a full-time worker and giving each job sharer a 1-week paid vacation. Health insurance premiums could be half covered rather than fully covered, or certain coverages selected up to a maximum cost.

A possible problem is conflict between job sharers. This can be greatly reduced or eliminated by good planning in the first place. Very important is to define each sharer's duties and responsibilities. Supervisors must also be involved in this process so that these people are integrated into the arrangements. Job sharers must be the types of individuals who are highly motivated, sincere and mature enough to assume these special obligations. They must be very willing to do their fair share. They must understand that their individual accomplishments will be evaluated as well as their teamwork.

Some Final Thoughts on Job Sharing

The responsibilities of the job and the assignments to be given to each of the two sharers must be carefully studied. Duties need to be evaluated to determine whether they will be joint or assigned to one or the other of the sharers. Equipment to be used needs to be considered and decided upon. Work schedules need agreement. Communication methods must be established. If sharers are to cover for each other in case of absences, then how this will be done should be decided upon.

The following can be used as a guide to making job sharing arrangements:

1. Such arrangements must be voluntary.
2. Equality with full-time positions must exist in fringe benefits, pay and job responsibilities all divided proportionally.
3. Full supervisor support is essential.
4. Co-workers must concur. Union approval is needed if the workers are unionized.
5. What is expected from the arrangement should be clearly understood by all who are involved.
6. Teams must be well organized, have adequate communication skills and be very cooperative.
7. Suggested time schedules are (a) morning/afternoon splits, (b) 2½ days each week, (c) every other day, and (d) every other week. The choice of schedule depends on the requirements of the particular job.

More flexibility in the workplace seems to be a growing management trend (Graham and Titus 1979). By job sharing, employers can tap a larger pool of potential employees. There is no valid reason why all employees should be on a rigid 40-hour work week. Many advantages can accrue to a foodservice that reaps the benefits of having at least some of their staff composed of competent, enthusiastic and highly productive job sharers—or those with other alternative work options.

EMPLOYEE'S HEALTH, NUTRITION AND ATTITUDES

Health and Nutrition

Good health and good work are more often than not synonymous. To be effective on the job requires alertness, good outlook and vigor to do the job in a safe and competent manner. During the period of indoctrination, a good training component is to impress upon the new employee the importance of maintaining good health and vigor, pointing out that getting 4 hours of sleep prior to beginning work is no way to function. In fact, lack of sleep is a major cause of accidents among workers.

One way to improve the worker's health is to provide good nutritionally balanced meals on the job. Improving the worker's knowledge of nutrition is an important part of his/her growth as a well-rounded person. Much can be learned by any foodservice employee that will be valuable for life. A helpful and concerned manager can encourage all of the staff to learn about good eating habits and keeping their health at a high level of efficiency.

Attitudes

An employee's attitude toward the job can be defined as how the employee sees that job in relation to his/her life as a whole. Many employees will be young people working in the foodservice as a means to an end—a way to make money for tuition or meals while they study for a career which may be entirely different than that of the food business.

A manager *can* influence an employee's attitude toward the job. Attitudes can be changed and structured to favor the employer by (1) providing incentives intended to produce an enthusiastic and helpful worker, (2) by strengthening beliefs of the worker in the integrity and sincerity of the manager, (3) by building a high level of trust between the employee and the manager, and (4) creating between manager and worker a feeling of friendliness which is genuine and felt mutually. As time passes these four factors can be constantly improved and built upon by intelligent and competent management.

An effective manager constantly keeps in mind that attitudes are very important and can be structured and improved by good management practices. Such a policy is fundamental to creating the kind of good employee attitudes that are so desirable. The manager must first have the best possible attitude towards the job and then try to reflect this by the practices that help build the proper attitudes in every employee.

Employees in contact with the public need to be reminded that their attitude is very apparent to the customers and guests. Customers are quick to detect an employee's attitude when they are being served, for example. The employee with a pleasant and enthusiastic attitude will reflect this in the dialogue being conducted, and if the attitude expressed is a wholesome and enthusiastic one, a bigger sale is likely to be made to a happier customer.

BETTER USE OF UNDERUSED PEOPLE

Quite commonly, there are people who simply are just not being used to their full capacity. They have talents of one kind or another or combinations thereof that simply are not being wholly used. There may well be people who are assigned to one job but who would be much more effective if assigned to another. Potential improvement in the productivity of the foodservice exists by considering better uses of staff members. This concept deserves more attention than it usually gets. The best way to discover this is to have a private talk at least twice each year to get to know each one of the employees as well as possible. The manager needs to ask questions and find out what the employee's interests and ambitions are. If the employee has certain interests, aptitudes, and ambitions that have not been fully clarified, the manager should discover what these are and create opportunities for improvement and achievement.

Having such a personal conference with each employee makes possible the identification of some of these unmet ambitions. Also, the manager could suggest to the employee possible job alternatives, such as rotating some job assignments, which might bring out these hidden interests and abilities.

Examples. (1)   A waiter/waitress would like to make sales calls for developing group business every afternoon or on certain days during the week. This special sales assignment might develop some very fine marketing talent that had not been utilized until the employee was given an opportunity to try this kind of employment.   (2)   The manager has to be out of town for a certain length of time. Putting someone else in charge and assigning new responsibilities during this period provides opportunities to bring out such talents and helps to more fully utilize particularly capable members of the staff.

REFERENCES

COHEN, A. and GADON, H. 1978. Alternative Work Schedules: Integrating Individual and Organizational Needs. Addison-Wesley Publishing Co., Reading, MA.

GRAHAM, B.C. and TITUS, P.S. 1979. The Amazing Oversight, Total Participation for Productivity. Amacom, NY.

FRESHWATER, J.F. and BRAGG, E.R. 1975. Improving food service productivity. The Cornell Hotel and Restaurant Administration Quarterly 15, 12–18.

LANE, H.E. 1976. The Scanlon plan: A key to productivity and payroll costs. The Cornell Hotel and Restaurant Administration Quarterly 17, 76–80.

SCHULER, R.S. 1981. Personnel and Human Resource Management. West Publishing Co., St. Paul, MN.

Selecting Employees

FINDING EMPLOYEES

Here are several recommended methods for obtaining good employees:

1. Prospective employees can be referred by the present staff. Experienced employees know the business and know the kind of person that is needed. They can help locate someone who comes closest to filling the job specification.

2. If it is not possible to secure applicants from employee referrals, one can notify the nearest Employment Security Commission office. They have employees available and can send qualified applicants. Or it may be desirable to use an employment agency and/or contact the local high school. There are many job seekers in the young people's group. The same is true in the older age group.

3. For unionized establishments another method is to seek employees from the local chapter of the Hotel and Restaurant Employees and Bartenders International Union.

4. Or a classified ad, completely describing the job, can be placed in a newspaper.

Young People

Many high school graduates will be looking for employment during the next decade. Here are some tips on going about hiring young people:

a. A talk with the high school principal concerning student employment will get suggestions for candidates for jobs.
b. Those with favorable records and high intelligence quotient ratings can be chosen.
c. When talking to several applicants, the job offer should be complete. Do not be surprised if an 18-year-old asks about the details of the retirement program!
d. It is important to insist on high standards of performance, appearance, and above all, a pleasing personality.

Some of the positions for which young people are particularly well suited are cooks, bakers, buspeople, waiters, waitresses and cashiers.

Older People

Many who are 65 years of age or older are in excellent physical and mental condition. They can be of great value to your business in several capacities. Persons over 50 who are seeking jobs or are retired early from other fields of work are likewise good potential employees.

Older employees have mature judgment and poise which are valuable assets. They are typically dependable, anxious to do a good job, neat in appearance and loyal.

Recruiting Enticements

Foodservice employment has many desirable and attractive features that can be used in recruiting. Foodservice establishments are pleasant, clean places to work. Tempting and well-balanced meals are provided without cost (or at a discount) to the employees. The decor of most places is stimulating and produces warm, friendly surroundings.

If one works in the kitchen, ability and knowledge of foods gained there will be valuable throughout life. In other positions, the increased knowledge can be transferred to other types of employment, which may be undertaken later in life. Many foodservice jobs are well paid and promotions are typically a very real possibility for many on the staff. There is a constant, if not growing, need for people who are skilled in the various occupations associated with foodservice. Also, it is a universal occupation so that jobs would be available in other localities, should the worker wish to relocate. Working with people is a valuable experience and this is an asset to many other types of employment where personal relationships are an integral part of the job.

INTERVIEWING, SELECTING EMPLOYEES AND AFFIRMATIVE ACTION

Personal Interviews

The personal interview of a prospective employee is an important method for obtaining information about this applicant. However, it really is not a particularly good procedure for making employment evaluations. This is because it is too subjective. Aptitudes, achievements, personal interests, and employment aspirations are more reliably determined by paper and pencil tests or situational tests. However, due to the legal complications in using written tests, many companies have even increased their reliance on the personal interview, despite its recognized limitations.

Preparation for the interview should be made in advance to be sure that all of the pertinent bits of information will actually be obtained. A check list should be at hand and notes taken as the interview progresses. A job description and job specifications should be available so that all aspects of the job can be covered in the interview. What qualities and abilities must a person have to succeed on this job? Experience with this position has indicated that there are certain special qualities and abilities needed for effective performance. Such aptitudes are termed *success predictors*. It is important not to omit essential information. There should not be an overlap of the same kind of coverage on the second and the third (and final) interviews. These last two interviews should bring out all of the remaining needed information for a hiring decision. Some jobs may require only one or two interviews.

Using one trait of the applicant to influence other qualities should be avoided. Sometimes a "halo" effect is created wherein one or two outstanding qualities of the applicant such as appearance and personality overshadow all other attributes. Thus, some important qualifications are neglected during the interview. Figure 1 illustrates the recommended steps in the selection of employees. Each of these steps should be carefully taken to help ensure that all needs will be sufficiently filled by the best available employees.

The following suggestions should be helpful in improving interviewing:

1. When interviewing each applicant, only job-related information should be obtained. It is important to use the success predictors which must be fulfilled by the one who is hired.

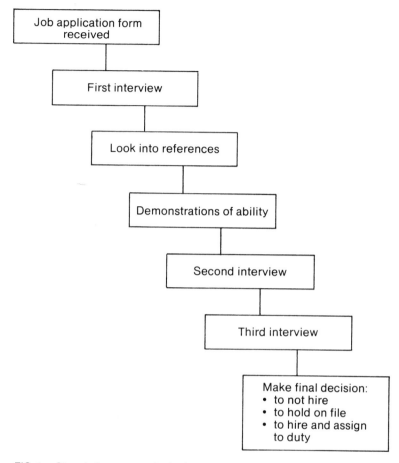

FIG. 1.   Steps in the process of selection and hiring. *Comments:* A printed application form is suggested. Each applicant should fill this out. How well this is accomplished is an early indication of capability. Third interviews are only given to those who have the best qualifications.

2.   Past behavior should be carefully brought out, since it will importantly affect future behavior. For example, if the applicant has had a large number of jobs over the past few years, it is likely that this applicant, if hired, will not stay with you very long either. However, you cannot use past experience as a predictor of what an individual will do on the job as a *legal* basis for selection or rejection.

3.   Nonverbal messages are also quite meaningful in an employment interview. Such factors as body stance, tone of voice, where the applicant sits on the chair, what is done with hands, appearance, hair style, dress, eye contact, way of walking, eyebrow movements, and quick movements can tell the interviewer quite a bit about the applicant. Eager, responsive and

positive individuals are typically much better bets than slower, less alert applicants.

Characteristics to Observe

The main indicators of job success are character traits and behavior traits. These include such important factors as a *positive attitude* toward the job being sought. The applicant should have a strong desire to contribute to the success of the foodservice as evidenced by his/her reply to such a question as "What do you think you could contribute to us here in this restaurant?"

Additional important factors include evidence of *motivation*—a desire to get ahead and work towards an employment goal. Other factors are *stability* evidenced by the number of jobs held in the past year or so and maturity shown by indications of *reliability* and *willingness to assume responsibilities*. *Intelligence* is hard to judge, but the manner in which questions are answered and such indications as the applicant's ability to *act with purpose, think rationally*, and *deal effectively* with his/her environment provide good evidence.

These characteristics are typically hidden behind outward appearance. Talking to the applicant for a few minutes and using visual appraisal will not bring out this vital information. A well-planned interview designed to reveal these qualities and the applicant's work history is the only way to help ensure that the right person is hired. An applicant's past history is the best indication of how this individual will perform in a new job. Hard workers in the past will be hard workers in the future. If *leadership* is needed, one should consider an applicant who has exhibited leadership qualities in the past. It is the job of the interviewer to draw out from the applicant the qualities that are vital to good employee selection.

Good Interviewing Techniques

The interviewer should be sure that the candidate is seated comfortably, and the interview should be conducted in a dignified and private environment. Recognizing the importance of the interview it should be planned for in advance and questions should be ready. It is important to make the interview conversational, friendly and outgoing, and to frankly ask the applicant to tell everything that would indicate that he/she is the right one for the job being filled (Schuler 1981).

The applicant should do about 80% of the talking and the interviewer 20%. Every opportunity to talk freely should be given the applicant. Questions should be open ended, such as "What jobs have you held over the past 2 years?" and "Why did you quit your last job?" Leading questions in which the answer is given should *not* be used.

Any indications of advising or criticizing should be avoided. Otherwise much of the free flow of information will be stopped and the interviewee will be very cautious as to what he/she divulges.

All of the applicant's statements should not be accepted at face value. If a particularly important statement is made, the applicant should be asked to support it with enough information to prove its validity.

The interview should bring out other qualities important to job success such as the candidate's attitude, motivation, stability, maturity, aptitude, and temperament. Studying the interview notes afterward should produce a reasonably good appraisal of the applicant's qualities that are suitable and necessary for the job. An evaluation of his/her predictors for likely success in the organization should be made.

For some types of jobs, an actual demonstration of ability may be required.

Some Final Suggestions

All three interviews should be coordinated together in a systematic manner to avoid stereotyped and quick decisions. Managers should always be involved in the selection process. If the department manager or supervisor is responsible for personnel matters, this responsibility can be used as the first step in selecting the individual. Then a final approval or rejection can be made after the general manager has interviewed the individual. Or the third interview could be made by the manager and supervisor together. If they both agree that this person is the best one, then this is likely to be a good decision.

Interviewing Applicants and Affirmative Action

The following types of questions are illegal:

- Marital status, including spouse's name
- Need for baby-sitting or child care
- Whether pregnant
- Weight and height
- Eye color or hair color
- Educational attainment
- Ever been arrested
- Age
- Credit rating, any pay garnishments, home or apartment ownership
- Availability for Sunday or Saturday work

Not all of these questions are in fact discriminatory, but some of them tend to reduce equal employment opportunity because they are not strictly related to the job. Any questions used in job interviews should be carefully evaluated as to whether they actually relate to job performance. Also, are they likely to result in subjective interpretation? Do they tend to reinforce old stereotypes? Do they tend to discriminate against minorities or women? Any questions with these types of flaws should be avoided (Kohl and Greenlaw 1981).

Affirmative Action and Employee Selection

In selecting employees, it is important not to discriminate on the basis of race, national origin, color, religion or sex. The Equal Employment Opportunity Commission established guidelines pointing out that tests used for selection be job related. The only way that job relatedness could be proved was by validation procedures—a comparison of test scores with job performance. However, in the 1978 guidelines, validation is not required in all cases. But, to avoid adverse impact in the selection process, the hiring decision rate for any minority group must not be less than 80% or the so-called bottom line criteria. What this means is that if one were to receive and test a group of applicants for positions in a certain category and hired 25% of the white applicants, one must also hire 20% (80% × 25%) of all blacks who apply and 20% of all women or other protected groups who apply. So doing proves that the tests administered or other criteria used do not discriminate against these groups. A hiring organization does not have to meet the 80% rule if it can demonstrate that all procedures used in selecting employees are job related. It is wise to keep on file data to show the number of applicants received and hired listed by race and minority group. Also one should keep copies of interview sheets to prove that the questions asked and answered were directly related to the job and were bona fide predictors of job success.

Handicapped Workers

The training officer of a large foodservice chain once remarked that one of the most productive and reliable workers in the entire organization was a handicapped dishwasher in their most successful unit.

This observation emphasizes the value of hiring persons who may be very well qualified for a job—yet are considered to be physically or mentally handicapped when initially interviewed for a position. A handicapped person is defined as one who has a mental or physical impairment which limits that person's activities. Also considered handicapped are those who have had a history of impairment or appear to have impairments when being interviewed. Under federal affirmative action laws, employers are required to act affirmatively to employ and to promote qualified handicapped persons and to adjust personnel procedures to help accommodate them.

When interviewing handicapped applicants, notations should be made in the person's folder that this individual is handicapped. Also, the results of the interview should be noted to document whether the person was hired or not hired. Reasons should be stated if the handicapped person was rejected, with a statement comparing the qualifications of the handicapped applicant with the person who was hired. If the handicapped person was hired, then include a statement of any special arrangements and accommodations that were made by your organization to help the handicapped person to be successful on the job. These procedures are advisable to comply with affirmative action laws in case there should be a compliance review of your employment practices. (For further information, see Morgan 1979.)

JOB ANALYSIS

Any organization must have the right types of people for achieving its goals. Good planning will result in determining the specific personnel needs. Part of this planning requires job analysis. The job analysis consists of three main functions: job descriptions, job specifications, and job evaluations. Before these functions are reviewed, however, one must keep in mind that the selection of staff is more than just fulfilling the specific needs of the organization. It is important for the manager to recognize the needs of each applicant and try to match the job with these needs. Also, the manager should try to match the rewards offered by the job to the applicant's aspirations, dreams, and hopes. So doing will benefit the long-range interests of the organization and the individual worker.

JOB DESCRIPTIONS

Keep the description short and to the point, and answer the following questions:

1. Worker's responsibilities?
2. Standards of performance? Supervision?
3. Methods worker uses? Equipment used?
4. Relation to other jobs? Job combinations?
5. Particular skills required?

Benefits of writing a job description now become apparent. These include the following:

1. Helps to establish a fair wage rate for the job.
2. Determines the amount of training needed.
3. Clarifies the qualifications required by applicants.
4. Shows supervisors what is entailed in performing the job.
5. Defines the job; reduces job conflicts and confusion.

A job description answers the questions, "what?" "why?" "how?" and "skilled needed?" Such criteria are needed for all job descriptions. (See samples in Appendix A.)

The job description should be prepared carefully. In unionized businesses, many union members will refuse to work outside of their job description. Therefore, it should cover all possible duties of that particular job.

When to Use a Job Description

As already mentioned, if a foodservice is unionized one undoubtedly will have to use job descriptions. If job descriptions are used, they should be written by either the supervisor or the manager. There is no point in writing a job description unless it accurately describes the duties of the particular job. When interviewing job applicants, one should use the job description for the position being filled.

Managerial jobs at higher levels should never have job descriptions (Townsend 1970). People in these positions have to use their best judgment in numerous instances every day and it is impossible to write a job description for someone who is a creative ambitious individual looking for every opportunity to contribute to the welfare of the organization. Situations and conditions in this business change very rapidly. A job description that is written at a particular time for a manager might very well go out of date when new methods or new procedures are incorporated into the foodservice because of rapid changes in equipment, food items, methods, etc.

JOB SPECIFICATION

This is a consideration of the details of what the job requires in terms of the individual who might be assigned to the position. The following are typical details:

Job title; department; sex; physical requirements of the applicant; working conditions; equipment, materials and tools used; compensation; training required; vacation policy; experience required; personality requirements; judgment; manual dexterity; accuracy; strength; supervision; responsibility; and opportunity for advancement

There may be others. The job specification should also be available to the interviewer when talking to an applicant.

JOB EVALUATION

This procedure determines the correct relative value in terms of pay rates for each job. For example, should a cashier receive more pay than a supervisor? The only fair way to judge is by using the job evaluation technique. Here is the method:

1. On a sheet of paper, construct a chart listing the primary qualities expected in persons who hold a particular job. For example, you might list education, intelligence, capacity for receiving instructions, experience, appearance, and other criteria down the left side of the chart. Across the top list a series of numbers, usually from 1 to 10. (See Fig. 2.)

2. Now rate each of the criteria according to its relative importance. Number 1 will be of least importance and number 10 of greatest importance. Keep in mind that you are evaluating the various qualities for what they "ought to be" rather than what they may be at the present time. Also remember that *it is the job*, not the person currently holding that job, which is being evaluated. Use a separate chart for each job. The ratings will be entirely a matter of judgment and therefore are not at all scientific. Howev-

Criteria	1	2	3	4	5	6	7	8	9	10
Education										
Intelligence										
Capacity for receiving instructions										
Experience										
Initiative										
Personality										
Adaptability										
Team worker										
Dependability										
Response to supervision										

FIG. 2.   Job evaluation chart. *Comments:* A fresh copy of the chart should be used for each position being evaluated. For example, the first evaluation can be of the position of cashier followed by the middle management supervisors or any other positions considered more or less on the same level. In using the chart, one checks the appropriate column from 1 to 10 for each criterion. Then one adds up the total score. Jobs with the higher score points should receive higher pay. (Different criteria than those shown may be used.)

er, whether you are overly lenient or not does not really matter, because the job evaluation is a matter of *relative* standing between jobs.

3.   Next, plot the jobs and the wage rates on a graph with the score point values along the bottom of the graph and the present wage rates on the left-hand side. A series of dots will result. These are illustrated in Fig. 3. Note that considerable variation exists in the placement of dots. If the importance of all of the jobs were ideally related in terms of the pay, the dots would form a straight line. They are not and thus some of the jobs are overpaid and some are underpaid.

4.   While a simple procedure would be to raise those who are underpaid and cut those overpaid, this is not practical. A better approach is to try to raise the pay of those who deserve it whenever possible, not give any raises to those overpaid, and when new employees are hired, hire them at the proper pay for the job, in accordance with the job evaluation. This procedure results in the most equitable system of pay for the jobs in the foodservice organization.

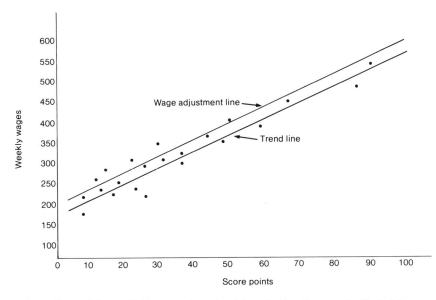

FIG. 3.   Determining equitable wages based on job evaluation. *Comments:* Each dot represents a job. The general trend is shown by the parallel lines. The wage adjustment line provides an area of wage variation within which wages would not be changed. However, if a worker was being paid at a rate above the variation range area, this worker would be continued at that rate. If a replacement were to be hired, then this new worker would be paid at the rate indicated by the trend line and the variation area.

JOB QUALITIES

Part of the work environment is how the employee looks at the job. Every job in the foodservice has certain unique qualities that distinguish it from the other positions. The specifics of any particular job are spelled out in the job description and the job specification. However, from the worker's viewpoint there are broader considerations which are discussed under the following headings:

1. *Job load.* This factor comes in three sizes—just right, too high and too low. Either of the latter two can produce stress and unhappiness in the employees. An important personnel function is to match worker and job so that the ability and aptitude of the worker is compatible with the demands of the job. What would be too high a work load for one person would be just right for another, or could be too low for someone else. It is important to match the worker in relation to his or her needs to obtain the closest fit.

2. *Security of the job.* Unemployment is a real fear and hopefully the job produces the opportunity for reasonably steady employment for the holder. Assuring the employee that a layoff is unlikely is a vital factor in building satisfaction and avoiding stress in the worker.

3. *Working conditions.* The actual environment in the foodservice is of very real concern to all employees. Often, workplaces are somewhat dull and unattractive and not very well furnished. An employee gives considerable importance to physical health, sanitation and comfort. Aesthetics can also be important to many workers. A psychological environment exists also. If the workplace is a happy and friendly place, this gives reassurance and support to the employee, particularly a new hire. Efforts to create and maintain favorable working environments for staff are good investments in employee satisfaction and productivity.

4. *Job characteristics.* How the job is structured bears on the employee's perception of how the job satisfies needs and wants. If the job has variety, significance, autonomy, identity, meaning, possibilities for favorable feedback, and order from the worker's viewpoint, then it is more likely to provide for the worker's needs than one more rigidly structured and routine.

PLACEMENT

Fundamental to good placement is the establishment of job success predictors for any specific job. In other words, one should make a list (on paper or in the mind) of the qualities needed in an applicant to quite well predict future job success. For example, it is known from experience that students of nursing in a large university near the foodservice become the best wait-resses. They are very clean and neat in appearance, have high standards of sanitation in their work stations, and are typically much concerned for the welfare of others and want to help them.

Good placement can also be made on the basis of several predictors. An applicant may be somewhat lacking in one or more predictors, but is very strong in still another. In the right job, this applicant will probably do very well. Or, an applicant may be lacking in one predictor but fine in the others. This applicant would do well if placed where the strong predictor is the dominating one.

What some people lack in ability, they make up in ambition and enthusias-tic motivation. Thus, one quality can compensate for another which might not be as strong as desired for that position. With excellent supervision, good training and continuing education efforts, this employee may develop into a very valuable asset to the foodservice.

TESTS

One method of evaluating job applicants is to give them tests that measure achievement, aptitudes, organizational ability, reasoning power, intelli-gence, clerical ability and cooking, baking, mixing or other proficiencies. Technically speaking, a "test" includes all scored or measured methods of appraising the applicant for job suitability.

It is important to remember that tests have become subject to legal constraints (affirmative action implications) when used to make hiring de-cisions.

There are three types of test validity that are recognized: (1) empirical, (2) differential and (3) content (Schuler 1981). The empirical is a measure of how well the test predicts performance of the applicant on the job. Differen-tial validity is a measure of the difference that occurs between what is indicated from the test results and the test taker's actual performance on the job. A predictor may be valid for one person and not valid for another. Such a difference is called a differential validity. Content validity refers to predic-tors that measure skills, education, learning, information, or ability related to those that are needed to do the job well. In order to demonstrate the content validity of any test it is very helpful to know the dimensions of the job, qualifications for successful performance, and the performance criteria such as speed of production, capacities, standards or similar measures.

Whether to use tests or not depends on the employment situation in the community and the availability of skilled personnel. Also because of legal constraints, the use of tests, especially written ones, has tended to decrease. Tests can only be used if they are reliable predictors of job success. It is advisable to have some kind of proof that this particular test does indeed predict subsequent success on the job. This is due to the legal implications of using tests to make hiring decisions. On the other hand, after the person is hired, any tests which help to place the new employee or to determine promotion or assignment to another better paying job are perfectly normal and acceptable.

REFERENCES

KOHL, J.P., and GREENLAW, P.S. 1981. National-origin discrimination and the hospitality industry. The Cornell Hotel and Restaurant Administration Quarterly 22, 26–29.
MORGAN, W.J. 1979. Hospitality Personnel Management. CBI Publishing Co., Boston, MA.
SCHULER, R.S. 1981. Personnel and Human Resource Management. West Publishing Co., St. Paul, MN.
TOWNSEND, R. 1970. Up the Organization. Alfred A. Knopf, New York, NY.

6 Training and Supervising Staff

TRAINING, TRAINEES AND TRAINERS

Why Train?

"With a 150−400% employee turnover in the foodservice business, why should we bother to train anyone? They are only going to leave soon anyway."

This erroneous line of thinking needs some stout logic in favor of good training methods. The faster an organization trains its people and gets them productive, the better off the business will be. A well-planned and effective training program shows the new employee that the organization cares about its new people and wants to help them to develop their skills and ability to the maximum of their capacity (Ference 1982). Having such a program creates a very favorable, positive image in the mind of the new employee.

In most instances people do not have the skills that are needed to do the job. A good training program will reduce turnover and attract other quality employees. This results in higher sales volume and higher profits because of more skilled salesmanship on the part of customer contact people and a better product coming out of the kitchen. Management must try to develop a feeling of care by exhibiting an outward concern to make the new employee as productive as possible in as short a period of time as possible.

One final reason: Many people seeking foodservice jobs may be frustrated and even rude at times, because they do not know very much about the food business and cannot give good service. A foodservice organization cannot afford to give poor service to anyone and should not have impolite untrained people contacting guests or fellow workers. A good training program can overcome such deficiencies.

Determining Training Needs

A good way to determine training needs is to assess the progress of the foodservice toward establishing goals. If the progress is not very satisfactory, then some form of training is likely needed. A review of the human resources and their current status and level of productivity is the next logical step to deciding what deficiencies exist and how these can be alleviated by a good training program. Some of the measures of competence could be a review of productivity as expressed by the base ratio (employment cost divided by sales for a given period) as is done in the Scanlon Plan (see Chapter 7). Another would be measuring the employee's production in terms of the standards of performance for that particular job. Other factors that might be considered include the degree of employee turnover, perceived level of job satisfaction, number of grievances, and even the amount of losses, spills, dish breakage, pilferage and accidents. All of these conditions, when reviewed, can reveal where training is the most needed.

Training should not be thought of as needed only by new employees (Morgan 1981). Everyone needs more training from time to time, including the supervisors and managers. Continuing education is an important factor today in any type of work including the professions. If your investigation indicates clearly a need for training, by all means undertake the program with enthusiasm and good insight as to what the training is designed to accomplish.

What is Training?

Training is simply learning. Learning is changing behavior. When an individual behaves differently and does something other than what was done before, then something was learned. It is apparent. It may have been learned well or poorly, but the behavior that is seen is that which has been learned.

The components of any behavior can be singled out with study. Once isolated, they can be taught. Thus, you must first identify or describe the kind of behavior desired. When you have decided on the end product desired, the learning products to be taught to achieve the goal should become apparent. Their components can then be easily taught.

For instance, if a behavior goal is to produce a skilled waitress, then the separate learning products to be taught are singled out. These would be (a) skill in graciously greeting the guest, (b) hand–visual coordination, (c) concentration, (d) dialogue, (e) accuracy and (f) promptness. The components of these individual product skills are then taught. (See Fig. 1.)

Recognizing the Learning Categories

Learning, of course, is not confined to motor skills. Concepts and attitudes are similarly learned by training in behavior patterns. The whole realm of learning categories can be subdivided as follows:

1. *Psycho-motor habits (skills).* These include those manipulative–mental habits (learning) that are readily repeatable. Examples are teaching a cook how to make a good item correctly or teaching how to set a table. (See Fig. 2.)

2. *Cognitive habits (knowledge).* These include understandings of such things as cause-and-effect relationships, basic concepts, information and ideas. An example is teaching the effect of certain temperatures on food items.

3. *Affective habits (attitudes).* These include emotional habits (learning) involving likes, dislikes, fears, anxieties, values and appreciations. An ex-

FIG. 1.   Dining room manager briefs waiters on details of today's menu selection.

FIG. 2. Just how to fold napkins receives attention from waiters as part of their training program.
Courtesy of Michigan State University Foodservice

ample is teaching the waitress that warm hospitality, politeness, cleanliness and good service to the guest are of utmost importance.

These qualities that make up behavior are often interwoven. They may be learned separately, such as by instruction in the separate product skills required in cooking. But often they are learned together. The waitress who learns to have a positive attitude toward cleanliness and service (affective) is also learning how to serve a dinner skillfully (psycho motor), and at the same time understanding why politeness and prompt service are so important (cognitive). The desired end product of behavior has been achieved— an efficient, productive waitress.

Trainers

Typically it is the supervisor who does the training. But, is this supervisor a good trainer? Knowledge and the ability to effectively *transmit* knowledge are two very different things. If the supervisor is not a particularly good trainer, then someone else who is very good at it can be designated as a trainer when needed. Furthermore, the trainer must know the absolutely correct way of doing any particular task. The learner will only learn methods that are taught. If the trainer really does not know how the job is correctly performed, then it will not be done correctly by the learner. All the learner will learn is what he/she was taught—right or wrong (Nebel 1978).

A good training method is to use the "buddy" system. Here, the trainee is turned over to a worker who really knows how the job is to be done. The learner sticks with the "buddy" until the job is thoroughly learned.

Planning the Training Program

As a business manager plans for a desired result, such as complete satisfaction to the guest, increased sales, greater profit, or reduced expenses, so must every teacher plan for the desired learning product or result—behavior.

In teaching, *these desired learning products are the managerial objectives.* For example, when a new employee is hired, the first objective in the management process will be training: "Now we will have to *train* him/her to do the job." New employees will always feel somewhat insecure during the first few weeks. They probably feel a need for growth and an opportunity to develop their skills and ability. A good training program tends to eliminate this margin of insecurity, and is a tremendous help to the employee. If a manager or supervisor does an outstanding job of training, he/she will be respected as a good "boss" and will build cooperation and teamwork among all of the staff.

The following is a successful course in instruction:

Who.   Determine if the learner has the capacity to learn.
What.   Analyze what is to be learned and in which sequence.
Why.   Help the employee find the reason to learn.
How.   Organize situations or activities in which learning is *possible* and *probable* and so prevent frustration as the result of failure.

Training Methods

Any manual or textbook that lists varieties of training methods would be extensive. In the next few pages we shall discuss seven commonly used and effective teaching techniques, beginning with job instruction training and dialogue training.

Job instruction training.   This is the traditional method used on most jobs and is familiar to most of us. (See Fig. 3.) It is useful for skill-type training—showing someone how to do something; for instance, training a cook to prepare an item (Gallagher 1977).

Dialogue training.   This is a new technique that creates realistic situations in which the accompanying dialogue is intended to teach. It usually has

FIG. 3.   Supervisor teaches correct use of convection oven.
Courtesy of Michigan State's School of Hotel, Restaurant, & Institutional Management

the triple effect of improving the actual ability (motor skill), deepening understanding (cognitive habit), as well as improving attitude (affective habit).

Following these types of training methods are discussions of *role playing, conference training, group instruction, apprentice training* and *on-the-job training*. Each of these has a place in the training program, and the application of each will be explained.

Job Instruction Training

When a person receives a carefully worked out sequence of instruction from one who fully knows the job, it can be mastered in a surprisingly short time and results in a very acceptable piece of work. Following is a sequence outline, start to finish:

Sequence of instruction

Prepare the instruction. (Get ready.)

1.   Decide the behavior desired.
2.   Analyze the material. Use job description for the following:

Skill (psycho-motor) training: List important steps.
Information (cognitive) training: List key points, important facts, and minor points.

Attitude (affective) situations: List observed behavior, probable causes and possible solution.

3. Plan the training. Using the training schedule—decide *who* is to be taught *what*; *how* is it to be taught; *where* and *when* to instruct the performance that is expected.
4. Prepare to instruct. Review training checklist. Secure teaching supplies and equipment. Arrange workplace. Study job breakdown. Review the four basic steps to be used.

How to instruct   (Use four basic steps.)

Step 1.   Prepare the learner: Put learner at ease. State specific job. Find out what the learner knows about job. Develop interest and desire to learn. Organize material to be learned in correct learning sequence.

Step 2.   Present the material: Use the following sequence to present the material: Tell—show—demonstrate—then question the learner. Present one step at a time clearly, patiently, and in the correct learning sequence as just stated. Stress key points by emphasis and repetition. Present no more than learner can master at one time.

Step 3.   Try out under supervision: Have learner do job—correct errors. Have learner repeat and explain steps and key points. Question learner: Why? What? How? Continue until *you* know *he/she* knows.

Step 4.   Check on learning: Check on understanding and performance. Correct errors—reteach. Put learner on his or her own. Tell where to go for help. Taper off coaching to normal supervision. Your motto throughout preparation and instruction should be as follows: "If the instructor has taught, the worker can perform."

Dialogue Training

Foremost among the methods for achieving motivational results for customer contact employees as well as job know-how is that of dialogue training.

To put reality and creativity based upon sound psychological and educational learning principles into the training program, one uses dialogue. That is, one creates realistic situations involving relations between people, and then has participants discuss the dialogue that illustrates these situations. Dialogue eliminates the need for skits or play acting, and it does not have the disadvantages of these traditional training devices. It eliminates the trainee's embarrassment at play acting and it saves time. Above all, it trains people to think; it isolates and pinpoints the idea that the trainer wants to make. But the ideas come from the trainees, not the trainer.

Planning dialogue training. The first step in planning the use of dialogue training is to obtain verbatim transcriptions of conversations held on the job. The trainer posing as a guest may record dialogues with a waitress, or the waitress may be instructed to give some examples of dialogue between waitress and hostess or cashier. The dialogues usually used are samples of dialogues that need improving. Correct dialogues are used for selling campaigns.

After representative samples of actual situations have been collected (some sample dialogues are presented here), the next step is to carefully study and analyze the dialogues. One should look for situations that particularly point up needs, i.e., for giving the guest better service, showing more courtesy or using an improved sales approach. The trainer should be able to identify those phrases that embody the desired sales principles and hospitality techniques to be conveyed, that is, the desired hospitality message.

Dialogues finally selected for the first phases of the training program can be prepared on overhead transparencies so they can be projected on a screen. Or the dialogues may also be duplicated on paper. The trainees like to make notes about the dialogues and the written sheets provide a convenient way to do this. This also instills self-confidence in the trainees and encourages them to enter into the discussion. As noted, this method should influence the employee's *attitude*, improve *interest* and build *self-reliance*. It usually increases *enthusiasm* as well.

The discussion constitutes the most important and final part of the dialogue training, which is usually done with a group.

Training procedure. Here is the suggested procedure for the dialogue training:

1. Trainer presents a brief explanation of the dialogue situation prior to presenting the dialogue, and explains the learner's role.
2. Dialogue is presented on screen if such is available. Duplicated copies are handed out. Or, just the copies alone could be used.
3. Silent period ensues during which trainees study the screen and/or their copies of the dialogue. They *think about what was wrong* and *what should be improved*—the proper way to have conducted the dialogue.
4. Trainer now proceeds to ask questions of the group, such as the following: "What was wrong?" "Do you think the employee said the right thing?" "Was the guest satisfied?" "Could an additional sale have been made?" "Could the conversation be improved?" "How?"
5. Group members give their ideas as to how the dialogue should have been conducted. Trainer should try to involve *every person in the discussion*. If some do not speak up, they should be called upon and asked for their opinions.

6.   The trainer then presents a brief review of the dialogue and summarizes the consensus of the group as to what the *best way would have been* for handling the particular situation presented in the initial dialogue.

7.   The above steps are repeated for each dialogue used.

Some results.   The object of dialogue training is to teach employees to think about typical situations they meet on the job and about the best possible dialogue to use in that particular situation. Actually it is the fact that the dialogue training is based upon real situations between customers and employees and between employees and supervisors that makes it so interesting and enjoyable. No unrealistic material dulls the learners' interest. They enter into the training experience enthusiastically because they sense that the material presented is exactly what really happens. The interpretation of what would have been said and done makes a lasting impression on the mind. This type of thinking strongly motivates the learner to try to handle the situation "right" at the first opportunity which presents itself. Thus, dialogue training helps the trainee to understand a situation thoroughly, and so he/she becomes more confident, assured and capable.

It is important to remember though that the ultimate purpose of dialogue training is to give the guest and customer *better service.* Better and more satisfying service results in greater sales and profits.

Sample dialogues.   In order to furnish guidelines toward organizing a training program, four sample dialogues are provided here. They involve waitress and guest.

Dialogue 1—Knowledge of the menu

Waitress: May I take your order now?
Guest: I see you have lasagne on the menu. What is this dish, anyway?
Waitress: Well . . . ah . . . now I don't really know just what that is . . . let me go and ask the chef.
Guest: Never mind, I'll take a cheeseburger and a cup of coffee.

Dialogue 2—Making suggestions

Guest: What do you have special out there tonight?
Waitress: We have all kinds of good stuff.
Guest: I notice you have chicken cacciatore on the menu. Is it good? How does it look?
Waitress: Everything is good.
Guest: Bring me some of that chicken cacciatore.
Waitress: (No reply, writes notation on check and leaves table.)

Dialogue 3—Increasing sales through suggestions

(Guest escorts his best friend into a fine restaurant for dinner. There is an attractive display of wines near their table.)

Waitress: Are you ready to order now?

Guest: Yes, we would like that sirloin dinner for two, medium, with the chef's salad, baked potato and coffee.

Waitress: Thank you. It will take a few minutes to prepare your steaks.

Guest (to friend): (After waitress leaves.) I would have ordered wine, but she didn't ask me if we wanted any and I'll be darned if I'm going to beg her to sell us a bottle.

Dialogue 4 (Exemplary)—Responding to suggestions from supervisor

Hostess: Mary, Mr. Hanson (the manager) would like to increase the sales of soup and we are stressing this for the next 2 months. When you are taking orders, why don't you suggest a delicious cup or bowl of soup?

Mary: That's fine. Are we going to have a special card on the menu about the soup?

Hostess: Yes, there will be a different soup each day.

Mary (to the first guest the following day): We're featuring garbanzo soup today, have you ever tried it? It's delicious. . . .

Guest: Never heard of it, what's it like?

Mary: It's a Spanish soup. It has beans in meat broth and is flavored with chorizo sausage.

Guest: I'll take a chance, bring me some.

Other Training Methods

Role playing. Role playing is a training device in which the trainee learns by observing and taking part in a dramatization of actual problem situations. For example, a waitress pretends she is serving one of her fellow workers as a guest. Under the supervision of an experienced trainer, she learns to do and say things correctly by play acting the part.

Conference training. Conference training utilizes the technique of group discussion of problems and an exchange of ideas. It also affords an effective method of influencing the attitude of group members. Each person receives practice in influencing other members of the immediate conference group. This is a stimulating and rewarding experience for the employee.

Group instruction. Group instruction makes use of group classes. A competent instructor must be provided. This might be organized under the study program of the Educational Institute of the American Hotel and

Motel Association. This organization, located at Nisbet Building, Michigan State University, East Lansing, also offers a good selection of home study (correspondence) courses, books, and reprints available at nominal prices. University or college short courses or study of books and trade journals are additional ways of providing training and educational opportunities for employees.

Apprentice training.   Another training concept is that of apprentice training. (See Fig. 4.) This is an organized program consisting of the formal

FIG. 4.   Apprentice cooks receive valuable hands-on education and experience by sampling and evaluating a fish item.

study of prescribed training manuals or books, lectures and demonstrations, the showing of films, visits to suppliers, etc., in addition to understudy training under an experienced trainer. The apprentice learns by being an assistant for a prescribed period of time on the job in addition to classroom work.

On-the-job training.   Learning by doing is the most meaningful way to teach an employee. Listening to a description of the job and viewing training films are helpful to ensure top quality training. However, the actual doing is the culmination of any training system. This makes the most lasting and influential effect on the employee. So dialogue training, role playing and other progressive methods, while strongly recommended, must be supplemented by the learning–doing process itself.

Good supervision in the actual working situation is essential for good on-the-job training (Dahmer and Kahl 1982). How well does the supervisor or department head train? Has he/she taken instruction or attended a short course on training methods? It is one thing to *know* the job and another thing to *train* the employee. The trainer usually needs training in this role of teacher, administered either by the manager or by a professional educator such as a local school teacher. A manager with a large staff can often arrange a short course for his entire staff or, better, for a select group of supervisors, using the help of the state university or community college in cooperation with local school personnel. Supervisors or department heads who have received such instruction in teaching methods are then much better equipped to do an effective job of training the employees.

Training Continuity

Regardless of the methods used in any training system, every employee, supervisor and manager needs new educational experiences to constantly keep informed and increase knowledge and ability.

All training must be considered as only a part of a regular program of *continuing education*. New ways of doing things, new equipment, new processes, new materials and new food items are appearing constantly and must be taught. Few people can operate continually at top-notch efficiency. They tend to get sloppy or indifferent from time to time, and to develop bad habits through lack of good supervision. Progressive management must therefore provide every employee with the opportunity to study and improve. *A regular training program coupled with retraining is the answer to superior employee performance.*

An additional bonus of a continuous program is that more employees within the organization are prepared to accept jobs of greater responsibility. Because they were encouraged to undergo training and improve themselves, they are now ready to step into higher level jobs when needed.

Training Evaluation

The purpose of such an evaluation is to list items that are oftentimes areas of weakness in individual employees and that need to be strengthened by additional training.

The evaluation sheet is used only by supervisors. For instance, for a cook it would be used by the manager in cooperation with the chef. After some period of trial, particular weaknesses, if uncorrected, should be brought to the worker's attention. This should be done with the proper use of psychology by saying something complimentary about the person's work and then mentioning the weak spot. The thought uppermost in mind should always be: What can the manager do to further train the employee? Giving plenty of encouragement and understanding would be one way to show true interest in helping the trainee to become a superior cook in every respect (Folsom 1974).

It should be kept in mind that the end objective of the evaluation program is to create superior guest services through high quality personnel. This means employees who have received effective and imaginative training. Supervisors and managers must be as fair and impersonal as possible, trying to help all employees improve and make the most of their potentialities.

Job Instruction Training Check List

Can I, the manager, say "yes" in answering the following questions?

A. Get ready to instruct.

   1. Plan the training.
      In planning, do I know

      a. of the worker: YES   NO

      that he or she needs to learn a job? .... ____ ____
      the job he or she must learn? .... ____ ____
      what can he or she do now? .... ____ ____
      from his or her background and interests,
      what can be used in training? .... ____ ____
      how quickly he or she learns? .... ____ ____

      b. of the training situation:

      where instruction will be most effective? .... ____ ____
      when instruction can be arranged? .... ____ ____
      when instruction will be most effective? .... ____ ____

      c. of the job:

      what specific job operations are to be learned? .... ____ ____

the level of performance the job requires? .... ___ ___
how to do the job myself at that level? .... ___ ___

2. Analyze the material.

    Have I asked myself

    is the learning time available adequate to teach
    the job? .... ___ ___
    what type of breakdown shall I use? .... ___ ___

    If a manipulative (psycho-motor) skill—

    is the job title descriptive of job? .... ___ ___
    do I know where training should be done? ...... ___ ___
    do I know time required in training? .... ___ ___
    are training equipment and supplies available at
    training place? .... ___ ___
    are important steps arranged in logical order? .. ___ ___
    are all key points included? .... ___ ___
    has breakdown been checked against jobs? ...... ___ ___

    If information (cognitive) training—

    what type of information is needed? .... ___ ___
    for which purpose is it needed? .... ___ ___
    what time is required? .... ___ ___
    what equipment and supplies are needed? .... ___ ___
    what are the important steps? .... ___ ___
    what is the logical order of steps for the
    "purpose?" .... ___ ___
    what are technical names and minor points? .... ___ ___
    have I checked information needed against
    breakdown? .... ___ ___

    If an attitude (affective) situation—

    do I know the attitude needing correction? ...... ___ ___
    do I know the parties concerned? .... ___ ___
    have I considered the personalities involved? ... ___ ___
    have I considered the best time to discuss the
    problem? .... ___ ___
    have any needs for equipment and supplies been
    arranged? .... ___ ___
    how much time will be needed? .... ___ ___
    do I have all the facts on "observed behavior?" ___ ___
    have I considered all possible causes? .... ___ ___

have I satisfactory remedies to suggest? .... ___ ___
is situation still in the annoyance stage? .... ___ ___
have I considered all possible results of failure? ___ ___

B. Use of the four-step method

Step 1.   Prepare the learner.

Have I considered how

    to put him or her at ease—do I know   YES   NO

        what actions will put him/her at ease? .... ___ ___
        what interests can be aroused to get the
        participants on a cordial basis? .... ___ ___
        how to make a natural approach? .... ___ ___
        how I can make an honest and tactful approach? ___ ___

    to state the specific job—can I

        describe the job accurately and simply? .... ___ ___
        relate it to his/her work? .... ___ ___

    to find out what he or she knows about the job—
    do I know

        what experience he or she has had? .... ___ ___
        what to ask to find out what he/she knows about
        the job? .... ___ ___

    to develop interest and desire to learn—do I know

        the interesting features of the job? .... ___ ___
        the story of the job? .... ___ ___
        the importance of the job to success? .... ___ ___
        the need for the job in satisfying a natural desire
        or ambition? .... ___ ___

    to place the trainee in the most advantageous learning
    position—have I considered

        where he/she can more easily be helped by the
        manager? .... ___ ___
        where the learner can see, hear and get the
        "feel" of the job? .... ___ ___

Step 2. Present the material.

Have I considered how

to tell−show−demonstrate−question−do I know

what I shall "tell" and how? .... ____ ____
what I shall "show" and how? .... ____ ____
what combinations of various methods I shall use? ____ ____
the use I can make of visual aids and exhibits? ____ ____
how I can provoke thought through questions? ____ ____

to present one step at a time (clearly, patiently, and in correct learning sequence)—have I considered

how to explain steps clearly? .... ____ ____
the places at which the learner can go wrong and how to overcome them? .... ____ ____
the best approach to each step? .... ____ ____
the reasons for each step (if needed)? .... ____ ____

to stress key points—do I know

all the key points? .... ____ ____
how to show their bearing on the important step? ____ ____

to present no more than learner can master—do I know

the safety precautions? .... ____ ____
what the learner can master? .... ____ ____
the difficulty of the job to a beginner? .... ____ ____
how to present the job in a simple manner? .. ____ ____
how much to teach before asking for a response from learner? .... ____ ____

Step 3. Apply the learnings. (Try out under supervision.)

Have I considered how

to have learner do the job and to correct errors—do I know

how to provide adequate practice by the learner? ____ ____
what errors are commonly made and am I prepared to reteach them? .... ____ ____

to have trainee repeat and explain steps and key
points—am I sure

>   he or she clearly understands the steps and key
>   points? .... ____ ____

to question why–what–how—do I know

>   what questions I can ask? .... ____ ____
>   how my questions will affect the worker's
>   judgement of the job? .... ____ ____

to continue until I know worker knows how to do
the job—am I

>   prepared to insist on sufficient repetition to get
>   correct performance? .... ____ ____

Step 4.   Check on learnings.

Have I considered how

to check on understanding and performance—
do I know

>   if questioning is enough? .... ____ ____
>   if watching performance is enough? .... ____ ____

to correct errors or reteach—am I

>   prepared to stop the learner courteously and
>   reteach when making an error? .... ____ ____

to put him on his own—have I considered

>   how soon to put the trainee on his/her own? . ____ ____

to tell where to go for help—have I

>   decided to whom he/she should go? .... ____ ____
>   told the other person that the trainee may come
>   for help? .... ____ ____

to taper off coaching to normal supervision—
have I considered

>   how often to check on learner? .... ____ ____
>   making note on a calendar of gradually reduced
>   checking until it becomes normal supervision? ____ ____

that success of the worker in learning the job is
largely my responsibility? .... ____ ____
if I am ready to teach? .... ____ ____

EDUCATIONAL UPGRADING

One of the toughest management jobs is to maximize the employee's
sense of self-worth, esteem, and self-actualization relating to his/her job
situation. One solution to this problem is to adopt a policy of educational
upgrading. Firms in the public hospitality business must do this through such
programs as their own schools or on-the-job training programs. In addition
to these, there are valuable educational opportunities available in the foodservice business that will aid considerably in upgrading the enrollee's ability.
Participation in such programs develops the employee's self-esteem and
improves confidence and job satisfaction.

Persons selected for educational upgrading should be those who truly
possess the interest and motivation to succeed in such a project. An appraisal can only be determined after a reasonable length of time in your
association with such employees. When the right employee is discovered,
there are a variety of educational programs that can be utilized. One of
these is the National Institute for the Foodservice Industry (NIFI). This
educational organization was founded by the National Restaurant Association and offers a wide variety of educational opportunities. Copies of their
program can be obtained by writing to NIFI, 20 North Wacker Drive,
Chicago, Illinois 60606. The Educational Institute of American Hotel and
Motel Association is located in the Nisbet Building, 1407 South Harrison
Road, Michigan State University, East Lansing, Michigan 48824. This organization offers correspondence courses, home study, group study programs
and educational materials concerning a wide variety of subjects of major
importance to successful foodservice operations. The reader can write for a
published description of these materials.

Recommended procedure is to inform any candidate who might be involved in such a study program that upon successful completion, the cost of
the course or study materials will be reimbursed by the management. This
provides a built-in incentive to complete the course and achieve an educational upgrading for individuals who are so motivated. Encouragement of
such up and coming personnel means a great deal to them. A manager might
suggest certain types of counseling or perhaps a visit to a hotel and restaurant school or allow time off for investigation of educational opportunities.
Career days in high schools provide a good exposure of potential employees

(and students) to the foodservice field. Encouraging them to look into possibilities is good management. Participating in such events is a wholesome contribution to educational upgrading. The cooperation of foodservice organizations with hotel and restaurant schools by hiring part-time students and taking interns for summer employment or even a 6-month's internship likewise contributes greatly to the employee's educational development.

Attending foodservice shows and seminars is a positive method of developing interest in acquiring more knowledge about this industry and its possibilities for lifetime careers. Reading trade journals regularly is also very informative and educational.

EVALUATING EMPLOYEES

It is important to appraise an employee's performance twice each year. This is a check on how well the employee is doing, who in particular is responsible for doing the various jobs, and how well they are being performed. There are many purposes for making such employee appraisals and these are as follows:

1.   People who are ripe for promotion are readily identified.
2.   Compensation schedules are considered and evaluated for appropriateness for each individual.
3.   Deficiencies in a person's performance can be identified and a program set up for improving and eliminating these weaknesses.
4.   The evaluation determines the relative value of an individual's contribution to the foodservice and helps to assess individual accomplishments.
5.   There is some current feedback on how each employee feels about the job and how they are performing in relation to what is expected of them.
6.   The 6-month evaluation helps to determine what size staff is really needed or if a reduction or increase in staff may be required.
7.   The review is an occasion for good communication between the supervisor or manager and the employee, and this communication helps build confidence and morale.

Goal Setting for Employees

An important part of the evaluation process is to measure to what extent the employee has moved towards the attainment of his/her personal performance goals. These goals were likely established at the time of hiring or after the employee had gained some experience in the organization. The manager and the employee's supervisor worked with the employee to establish the goal or goals which that employee wanted to reach. How this level of attainment is measured will depend on the particular job. If the goals are not being sufficiently met, then a program to step up training or improve supervision or other measures should be formulated. Or, the goals may now be exceeded. Discussion is then held as to the next highest goal for which to strive.

In determining whether the employee has reached a certain goal or not, in some types of positions, *work standards* have not been established. The supervisor then makes an evaluation as to whether the employee has reached the desired standard or not. For example, your standard for a breakfast cook might be one cook for every 90 breakfast customers. A measure of this cook's productivity is then made to see if the standard has been reached.

Conducting the Appraisal Interview

In order to make the interview as accurate and meaningful as possible, here are some suggestions which should benefit the employee as well as the manager or supervisor:

1. Be sure to say something complimentary and encouraging to the employee at the outset. This praise creates a relaxed, pleasant, and friendly atmosphere in which to begin the interview.

2. State specifically why the interview is being conducted so there is no doubt in the employee's mind as to why this meeting is being held.

3. Encourage the employee to fully participate in the discussion. Any work environment factors that are affecting work performance should be brought out—either good or hindering. The employee hopefully will see this interview as a part of his/her development as an ever more valuable employee.

4. Clear up any misunderstandings as to what the job responsibilities are at this interview. Have the employee's job description at hand to settle any uncertainties about the employee's duties.

5. Consider any organizational goals if using the systems approach and/or some kind of group incentive program. Be sure these goals are clearly understood and their implications to the success of the organization made apparent.

6. Bring forth the employee's personal ambitions and aspirations and discuss his/her progress toward them with candor.

The Evaluation Sheet

An individual separate evaluation sheet should be used for each interview. When evaluating the employee, items should be listed that are oftentimes areas of weakness in this individual and that need to be strengthened. An additional use of this sheet is to point up items that should be covered in training.

For each employee, each item should be reviewed on the evaluation sheet and rated as "poor," "fair," "good," or "excellent," placing entries under the heading "present status." Without doubt a variety of ratings will be given and of course the objective is to eventually make them all "excellent." Figure 5 illustrates a form that could be used.

Employee's name _____ Department/Section _____
Job Title _____ Date hired _____
Date _____

| | Present status | | | | Progress |
	Poor	Fair	Good	Excellent	
Job understanding					
Attitude toward job					
Dependability					
Productivity					
Quality of work					
Adaptability					
Creativity					
Work dedication					
Comments					

FIG. 5.   Employee evaluation form. *Comments*: Use the form at 6-month intervals. Discuss both strong points (first) and then weak points with each employee. Employee should not have access to this form. Other criteria than those shown could be used.

No information concerning the rating should be given to the individual worker. After some period of trial, particular weaknesses, if uncorrected, should be brought to the worker's attention. This should be done with the proper use of psychology by saying something complimentary about the person's work and then mentioning the weak spots. The uppermost concern should always be what the manager can do to help the employee. Giving plenty of encouragement and understanding is one way to show sincere interest in helping the employee to become a superior worker in every respect.

During training no entries should be made in the "progress" column at the outset of the training program. As the program progresses entries, such as "some," "much," or "none," should be made. A weekly or monthly rating during the training period is suggested but this will depend upon the nature of the training program.

It is important to keep in mind that the end objective of the evaluation program is to create superior guest services through high quality personnel. This means employees have received effective and imaginative training. Individual favoritism toward any particular employee has no place in the rating process. Supervisors and managers must at all times be as fair and impersonal as possible. They must try sincerely to help each employee improve and make the most of his/her potentialities. An abundance of deficits found on evaluation sheets may reflect on the training and supervision rather than on the employees.

SUPERVISORS

The term supervisor as used here refers to an individual who manages those people who are not managing other people. Thus, a supervisor is the basic managerial element in the foodservice.

A good supervisor must be the following:

1. A balanced person
2. Cognizant of his/her role in sales
3. Guest or customer oriented
4. Technically qualified
5. Experienced
6. Employee-improvement minded

The supervisor is the member of the management team closest to the workers (See Fig. 6.). The supervisor must resolve the needs of each individual under his/her supervision in consideration of the goals of the organization. How well this is accomplished depends on the skills and

FIG. 6. Banquet manager reviews details of service with staff members preparing for a catering function.
Courtesy of Michigan State University Foodservice

understanding of human relations possessed by the supervisor. For further information see Haimann and Hilgert (1977) and Heckmann and Blomstrom (1981).

Selecting someone for the position of supervisor or department head is a very important decision. Equally important are the manager's efforts to improve the supervisor's ability. These are the real keys to success in managing the foodservice. About one-third of employee job changes can be attributed to poor supervision. The quality of supervision will largely determine the level of employee performance. Supervisors should be given the opportunity to occasionally brush up on improved techniques of leadership. Special courses in supervision are available from the Educational Institute of the American Hotel and Motel Associations. There are also similar courses available through the National Institute for the Foodservice Industry.

REFERENCES

DAHMER, S.J. and KAHL, K.W. 1982. The Waiter and Waitress Training Manual, 2nd Edition. CBI Publishing Co., Boston, MA.

FERENCE, E.A. 1982. Toward a definition of training. The Cornell Hotel and Restaurant Administration Quarterly *23*, 25−31.

FOLSOM, L.R.A. 1974. Instructor's Guide for the Teaching of Professional Cooking. Culinary Institute of America, Hyde Park, NY.

GALLAGHER, M.C. 1977. The economics of training food service employees. The Cornell Hotel and Restaurant Administration Quarterly *18*, 54−56.

HAIMANN, T. and HILGERT, R.L. 1977. Supervision: Concepts and Practices of Management. South-Western Publishing Co., Cincinnati, OH.

HECKMANN, I.L. and BLOMSTROM, R.L. 1981. Start Supervising. The Educational Institute, American Hotel and Motel Association, East Lansing, MI.

MORGAN, W.J. 1981. Supervision and Management of Quantity Food Preparation, 2nd Edition. McCutchan Publishing Corp., Berkeley, CA.

NEBEL, E.C. 1978. Motivation, leadership, and employee performance: A review. The Cornell Hotel and Restaurant Administration Quarterly *19*, 62−69.

BIBLIOGRAPHY

AHMA. (Reprint.) Profit Motivation, the Key to Waiter−Waitress Training. Educational Institute, American Hotel and Motel Association, East Lansing, MI.

U. S. DEP. OF HEALTH AND HUMAN SERVICES. n.d. Foodservice Manager Training and Certification Program. Public Health Service. Food and Drug Administration, Washington, DC.

KENT, W.E. (Reprint.) Taking the dread out of employee evaluation. The Cornell Hotel and Restaurant Administration Quarterly.

NRA. 1979. Sanitation Operations Manual. National Restaurant Association, Washington, DC.

Motivating Employees

INCENTIVE PROGRAMS

There are some basic principles that apply to any type of incentive program. Here are the essential concepts:

1. *Everyone is motivated in some way or another.* However, employees differ greatly in what kind of incentive program might motivate them. Basically, people will respond to any incentive program to the extent that they see the outcome as satisfying. What motivates one person tremendously may have only a mild effect on another. If a person in a particular incentive program sees a quite high probability of the program having a satisfying outcome, then this person will respond well and perform as intended. This employee perceives that by successfully exhibiting the behavior which management desires, he/she will likely reap the benefits in personal satisfaction and material reward (Nebel 1978). So, if any incentive program is to be successful for the foodservice, the desired behavior must be clearly spelled out. Then the rewards are likewise described if the employee (individual) or entire staff (group) performs as specified in the incentive program. (See Fig. 1.)

2. *There must be specifically stated objectives of the program.* What specifically should be accomplished? The objectives must be realistic and

FIG. 1. Good news! Department staff learns from supervisor that the goal for the month has been achieved!
Courtesy of Michigan State University Foodservice

achievable. Achievability is the key success word. For example, if the goal is to increase sales and profits, then what are the specifics?

    a.   Increase dessert sales 15%.
    b.   Increase total sales 10%.
    c.   Increase catering 5%.
    d.   Raise average check 12%.

   3.   *Participants should be influential.*   One way to decide on this is by asking "Who can influence the outcome or success of the project to increase sales (for example)?" Those who can should be the participants.

   4.   *The timing should be right.*   When should the program begin? For how long? (The program should be long enough to do the desired job, but short enough to keep your staff inspired.) Some are a matter of months, some a year or longer.

   5.   *The rewards should be timely.*   Awards should be speedy at the end of the campaign, or even continuous, if appropriate. Awards based on dollar amounts are the best as these can be accurately determined and reported to the participants.

6. *The program should be carefully developed.* You cannot get too much information when doing the planning. Good, workable rules that produce results are based on solid, factual, accurate, complete, reliable information and advice.

7. *Performance reports should be provided.* Participants must be kept informed of the progress toward the goal. These should be made at meaningful intervals. Program communications are a vital element in any incentive program. It is important to remind, educate, motivate, and inform everyone involved, and continue to do so. Each participant must know that there is this opportunity to earn an award for a certain level of performance. They should be convinced that they are capable of doing so—if they put forth that extra effort. They must believe that the extra effort is worth it because of the reward that they can earn.

8. *Product knowledge should be emphasized.* On-the-job performance can be improved by increased product knowledge. Some kind of a training program can be very helpful in increasing sales effectiveness, for example. (Review Chapter 6.)

Necessary Management Philosophy

If an incentive program is to be assured of success, there must be a management philosophy that embraces the need for increasing the scope of each employee's role in the foodservice. Any incentive plan necessarily increases the responsibility and involvement of all or most of the staff members. They must be concerned about achieving the goals and know that goal attainment will increase their incomes. A manager must truly believe that his/her staff possess unused potentials and abilities that can be unleashed and applied in the right direction. Also, a manager must see the staff as the foodservice's most valuable resource which can be considerably increased in value. This is accomplished by *additional education and training, more counseling, more personal attention, and by more praise, recognition, coaching, encouragement and friendship.* The manager says, "I want to make Kathy and Jack as good as I am." Such nonmonetary incentives are just as important as financial bonuses. In fact, they should *always* accompany *any financial incentive plan.*

If the plan is to be successful, it must be founded on the following four conditions:

1. *Identity.* The manager and his/her employees must truly believe that there is a need for change and that the resources of the foodservice can be managed more effectively.

2. *Participation.* Each employee must accept responsibility for the mandate and the opportunity to influence the success of the operation.

Participation includes accountability for one's own job and to all of the other employees. In other words, each employee must strive to achieve and not let the others pull the load.

3. *Equity*.   There must be a feeling of fairness and a balanced return that really benefits the guests or customers, the employees, the managers and the owners. Thus, when the plan is being created, everyone who is in any way involved should participate in the plan's development and approve of its final version.

4. *Managerial competence*.   There is an unequivocal requirement of the general manager and the supervisors to define and increase the climate for improvement and reaching the goals. Creating the plan and being sure of its probable success is a good challenge to the professional manager.

The Program Requirements

Whatever type of incentive plan is finally decided upon, it should have the following elements:

1. *The practice of cooperation*.   The heart of the plan is to cultivate a very high level of cooperation, achieved by the dedication of everyone to the established objectives. (See Fig. 2.) Each person must see "What's in it for me?".

FIG. 2.   Waiter and waitress exemplify teamwork in providing superior guest table service.
Source: Les Gourmet Club of Michigan State University

2. *The involvement system.* The details, timing, length, implementation and review of the plan are the concerns of all. Involvement and participation are essential. The plan should depend heavily upon employee suggestions for increasing sales and decreasing costs. (The specifics of each are to be spelled out in the plan.)

3. *The incentive formula.* Specifics of the plan in numbers (preferably in dollars) must be spelled out. The higher the achievement, the higher the bonus. Bonuses are always tied to performance.

Expected benefits (assuming a sales or profit-increasing plan) are as follows:

1.   Employees become much more willing to provide useful sales and cost cutting suggestions and ideas due to increased involvement.

2.   There is more interest in doing a quality job and making customers and guests want to come back again and again.

3.   There is a greater willingness to help each other and to share knowledge, methods and shortcuts. This enhances employee communication.

4.   There results an increased awareness of sales problems and the effects of competition.

5.   There is more recognition of the importance of increasing sales and raising the average guest check.

6.   There are fewer grievances, less absenteeism, and a lower quit rate.

7.   Employees and management collaborate to do problem solving. Thus, there is a better understanding of each other's limitations.

8.   Everyone becomes concerned about the success of the business.

9.   The incentive plan becomes a mechanism to unlock the full intelligence which exists in the employees. (It is amazing, sometimes, what employees can come up with in good ideas if they are really challenged to do so.)

10.   The involvement system is the most exciting element. All of your human resources are challenged to strive for and to reach full potential by reexamining work and goals. This benefits the foodservice, the employees, the managers and the customers who are the recipients of a more competent, enthusiastic and gracious foodservice staff.

Monetary Incentives

There are many different kinds of incentives. The most commonly used plans are the individual plan and the group plan. Under the individual level incentive plan, the plan is set up for a particular worker. For example, if a certain level of achievement is established for a job and the worker exceeds this level, then the worker receives an incentive payment representing a portion of this overachievement. An example might be a utility worker or maintenance man. If costs of maintenance could be reduced, say $500 in the year following establishment of the plan, he would receive 30% of the savings or a $150 bonus based upon this achievement.

Under the group plan, suppose that the average sales for a dining room were $50,000 for a particular period of time, say for the month of April. If during April of the next year the volume was $60,000 and menu prices had not been raised or portions increased, then say 35% of the profit on the additional sales would be divided up equally among all of the workers in that particular department.

Nonmonetary Incentives

There are also nonmonetary incentives. Saying the right thing at the right time can mean a great deal to employees. [See Hill and Stone (1977).] This nonmonetary system is known as "positive reinforcement." It lets the employees know how well they are meeting specific goals and gives them praise and recognition. As the employee sees it, good work is rewarded by recognition from his/her supervisor or manager in the form of kind words and statement of recognition of the employee's worth. Such rewards are very important to most employees. See Figs. 3 and 4.

FIG. 3.   Special Halloween cake for a staff party.

FIG. 4.   Having a pleasant room for coffee breaks is an important privilege for staff.

Other rewards, such as extra days off with pay, some kind of special privilege, a free meal for the employee and a guest, parties for the employees or athletic activities, give such recognition. To be effective, managers must use both monetary and nonmonetary forms of incentives. Incentives cannot be considered as optional. They are necessary in today's modern world of business. Competent, hard working employees are attracted and held by such incentives.

Managerial Incentive Plans[1]

Special consideration should be given to managers at various levels as well as to the general manager (Townsend 1970). Usually this takes the form of a cash bonus for the department or the foodservice business as a whole, if a specified level of sales or profits are achieved. Other possibilities are stock options at some prearranged price situation. Or there can be shares of stock tied directly to the achievement of established goals. Another variation is a combination of cash bonus and stock shares as a reward for good performance (Cauvin 1979).

---

[1]Additional information can be obtained from the Profit Sharing Council of America, Suite 722, 20 North Wacker Drive, Chicago, Illinois 60606.

Suggestion System

Somewhat similar to cash bonuses is an employee's suggestion system. Rewards of cash are made to those who make useful (and hopefully) profitable suggestions. Such a practice is recommended as some of the best ideas come from those who are in daily contact with the various operations of the business.

Work Group

If the incentive goals of a work group are clear and the group members are motivated, the attainment of the incentive program is all but ensured. Also, if the group's goals are synchronized with that of the foodservice as a whole, good results are even more likely. Managers can thus consider the influence of the group on individual employees as a key to achieving motivation toward the incentive goals.

BONUSES

When considering a bonus, first consider some of the principles involved:

1. A bonus is not pay.
2. A bonus should be considered as an extra reward for extra effort.
3. A bonus is an individual matter calculated for each person.

The objectives of a bonus plan are as follows:

1. Produce extra effort from participants. A bonus is always based on performance.
2. Favorably direct the efforts of each employee.
3. Provide extra compensation according to the success of the food-service.
4. Raise morale and enthusiasm of all of the staff.
5. More fully utilize the intelligence and capabilities of the staff.
6. Increase profitability.

When considering a bonus, the following procedure is recommended:

1. Consult an experienced C.P.A., advisory firm or foodservice consulting firm.
2. Talk over the basic concepts of a bonus plan with your supervisors and some key employees. Obtain their ideas and inputs. When the plan is

formulated, be sure it is clearly understood and meaningful to all employees. Enlist their support and enthusiasm.

3.   Make sure each employee judges it to be equitable.

4.   Make it be result oriented and reflect employee performance.

5.   Give high producers the big bonus and low producers a low bonus or none. This applies to service and sales personnel.

6.   Closely link the bonus in time to the performance upon which the bonus is based. Ideally, this would be a daily or weekly or monthly bonus. However, a quarterly or semiannual period is possibly more feasible from the accounting standpoint, and an annual bonus is also used quite often. But the sooner the bonus is tied to the performance the better.

7.   Make the evaluation as objective as possible. Such evaluation is usually done by a supervisor or the manager. All involved employees should be eligible and they should be able to periodically measure themselves during the year. This means that some kind of production or financial report must be available to each of the employees. Good communication is an essential element in operating a bonus plan. Be willing to listen to employee needs and concerns. It is possible to set up the bonus plan based on physical production such as number of covers per month or production per hour of salads or some other physical measure. However, as the name of the game is profits, it seems more logical to base the bonus plan on some kind of financial results rather than physical production. *For example*: A bonus for waitresses could be 20% of the average per person check over and above the average check for that week. Suppose the average check is $12.50 and a particular waitress had a check average of $13.50. The waitress would receive 20% of the difference of $1.00 which would be 20 cents for selling up on the menu. Such an arrangement works very nicely for service staff.

However, what about the kitchen staff? One foodservice organization provides a "kitty" made up of the 15% gratuities from each catering event. For each of such events, waitresses are paid $5 per hour with a minimum of 6 hours regardless of how long they work on any event. The pay which the waitresses receive comes out of the 15% gratuity. But there is a considerable amount of money left over in this "kitty." Every January 1 and June 30, this kitty is divided equally among all employees of the kitchen regardless of how long they have been on the job. (See also the first section in this chapter on Incentive Programs and the following section on the Scanlon Plan.)

SCANLON PLAN

The Scanlon Plan is a combination of management–employee relations philosophy and a group incentive system (Simmons and Mares 1983). This plan emphasizes employer–employee participation, sharing more in the operation and the increased productivity of the foodservice. This plan can be used in unionized as well as nonunionized organizations. The basic concept of the Scanlon Plan is that a bonus for the employees is determined on the basis of the savings in labor costs (Lane 1976). These labor costs are measured by comparing the payroll in relation to the total sales of the foodservice on a monthly or bimonthly basis. Past month's ratios help estimate labor costs for future months. The difference between actual costs and expected costs are shared by the employees. For example, the employees could receive 75% of the savings and the employer 25%. Because all of the employees share in the savings, one group does not gain at the expense of another. Each employee's bonus is determined by converting the bonus fund into a percentage of the total payroll and applying this percentage to the employee's pay for the month. It is apparent that the principal ingredient of labor savings cost is the efficiency of an employee's performance. Any suggestions that the employees can make to save labor costs and be more productive will be reflected in a larger labor cost savings. Consequently, a larger bonus will be paid to the employee at the end of the month. Thus, employee suggestions are vital to the success of the Scanlon Plan. The plan also provides a psychological plus as the employee now sees that ideas which will improve employee efficiency, when implemented, will directly benefit him/her in a higher income.

Benefits of the Plan

Here are the beneficial results expected of the Scanlon Plan:

1. The employees have motivation to come up with as many useful cost-saving ideas as possible.
2. The employees exhibit willingness to accept changes and to make work new equipment and methods that will increase productivity.
3. A better work place and work climate are provided.
4. There is an increased interest in the quality of work.
5. There is greater inclination for workers to help each other and share their knowledge of shortcuts.
6. There is less overtime or no overtime.
7. The employee insists on efficient management.
8. A greater awareness of sales problems and how to meet problems of competition exist on the part of employees.
9. Fewer complaints and grievances are noted on the part of employees.
10. A greater increase in productivity is observed.
11. There are fewer quits and consequently a lower turnover.

The Scanlon Plan is well adapted to the foodservice industry. It is an industry that does have quite a bit of opportunity to increase efficiency, especially when newer types of production equipment are put into use. Substantial savings can be accomplished, but this equipment must have willing, cost-conscious employees to operate it. That is where the Scanlon Plan concept comes in with its direct relationship of labor costs to the employee's bonus. These savings are then translated into increased pay for each employee. It can be readily seen that each employee has an incentive to increase efficiency.

Disadvantages of the Plan

There are also some disadvantages to incentive plans. From the managerial standpoint, there are somewhat more bookkeeping costs and administrative expenses.

From the employee's standpoint some employees might believe that incentive plans encourage competition among workers and the firing of slow workers. Also, some workers may feel that they do not receive their fair share of the increased productivity. Incentive plans are sometimes viewed as too complicated and many employees do not understand them. Standards are set unfairly. Some employees feel that incentive plans put a strain on the workers and this injures their health. Incentive plans are considered as management's way of avoiding giving pay raises. The plans force workers into doing more than a fair day's work. Some may be of the opinion that management put in the plan due to a lack of trust in the integrity of the workers.

These beliefs are all fallacies and with proper involvement of supervisors and workers in the formulation of the incentive plan at the outset, almost all, if not all, of these objections can be eliminated. When a worker believes that benefits result from another worker's performance, the worker is much more likely to encourage fellow workers to perform well. As a matter of indoctrination, sharing of planning and expressions of enthusiasm will help make these plans work. Incentive plans are a valuable and probably even essential part of good management today.

Hypothetical Example of a Scanlon Plan

Follow this example: Suppose an operation shows an average of 35% labor cost. This cost should include all employment costs such as contributions to Social Security, unemployment insurance, worker's compensation, insurance such as health or life plans paid for by the foodservice, vacations with pay, training costs, part-time help, employee's meals, payroll taxes and any other people costs. These employment costs are related to gross income which is that amount which represents the value of production. This is usually sales, but in some types of foodservices, it might be the value of all of the meals and beverages that were produced. A ratio is established by dividing the employment costs by the value of production or sales. Comparisons are made for each projected month with a comparable past month. January, 1985 estimates are based upon the actual experience in January, 1984.

To operate the plan, one must make an estimate of the sales (example) for January, 1985 based on the experience of January, 1984. It may be higher or lower than the month being compared. Then one takes 35% of this (example) to estimate employment costs for January, 1985. This relationship is called the base ratio, 35%. The next step is to determine what the actual ratio was at the end of January, 1985. The sales are summarized and likewise the employment costs. Any large items such as various kinds of employee insurance that sometimes are paid only once each year would be prorated by months for these calculations.

Here is an hypothetical example:

Average base ratio for the past three years = 35%.

For the immediate past year, one should calculate the base ratio by months to see if there is a wide fluctuation. For example, if January was 35%, February 43% and March 30%, it would be better to use the comparable ratio for each month rather than the average for the past three years. However, for this example, 35% as an average will be used.

January 1985 (Estimated):

$$\text{Sales} = \$84,000$$
$$\text{Employment costs} = \$29,400 \quad (35\% \text{ of sales})$$
$$\text{Base ratio} = \frac{\$29,400}{\$84,000} = 35\%$$

January 1985 (Actual):

$$\text{Sales} = \$85,117$$
$$\text{Employment costs} = \$28,009$$
$$\text{Base ratio} = \frac{\$28,009}{\$85,117} = 32.9\%$$
$$\text{Productivity} = \$85,117 - \$28,009$$
$$= \$57,108$$

Difference between estimated employment cost and actual employment cost is $29,400 − $28,009 = $1,391. The employee's share of this amount would be 75% or $1,043.25 and the owner's share 25% or $347.75. To equitably distribute the $1,043.25 among the employees, divide the January bonus of $1,043.25 by the employment costs for January—$28,009. Thus,

$$\text{Bonus percentage} = \frac{\$1,043.25}{\$28,009.00} = 3.7\%$$

Each employee would thus receive a bonus for January of 3.7% of his/her pay. For example, an employee earning $700 per month would receive a bonus of $700 × 0.037 = $25.90. Of course, the higher the productivity, the more bonus that would be earned. Employment costs could be reduced by using more automatic or higher productivity equipment, eliminating overtime, reducing part-time employees and working harder to handle increased business without hiring more staff. All employees would share in the bonus. There could be many variations of this procedure by determining who would be participating and how the bonus would be calculated and distributed. For more information on the plan, see Frost *et al.* (1974).

SALARY AND WAGE REVIEW

What a person is paid is usually the best indication of that person's worth to the organization. Pay is very important to the individual worker and salaries and wages are a major expense to any foodservice organization. Consideration of pay levels is one of the most important personnel functions. It must be done expertly to avoid internal conflicts and dissatisfactions (Wallace 1984).

There are two major considerations in determining pay levels: (1) the results of the work on job analysis (see the section on this in Chapter 5) to determine individual wage levels and (2) the pay levels of similar or competing organizations in the geographical area. Some companies have a policy of paying their employees 15% above the going wage in that area. They feel that doing so attracts a superior-type person and the increased efficiency and productivity are well worth the extra cost. (They are probably right.) In any case, the wage levels in your community do have a strong influence on your wage rates. A survey of local wage levels is needed by any manager when reviewing wage rates.

If your organization is unionized, the pay levels are negotiated under provisions of the union contract. Also federal and state minimum wage laws prescribe certain levels together with the various rules for exemptions.

Merit vs. Cost-of-Living Increases

It is important for employees to be convinced that superior performance will result in pay increases. An individual, personal, private conference with each employee twice each year is the best way to achieve a mutually satisfying wage and salary administration. At such a meeting, the manager reviews the performance of the worker and then informs him/her of any compensation change. One should be sure, however, that the employee clearly understands what good performance consists of, accepts these measures as fair and inclusive and observes that the best performers in the organization actually do get merit pay raises based on these measurements. If these conditions actually exist, most pay problems become less severe.

Cost-of-living increases have been prevalent over the past two decades, but they are not very good wage and salary administration. With inflation subsiding, such increases will likely be used by fewer and fewer firms. However, such increases are considered needed if the economic situation indicates that the employee's standard of living would deteriorate if a percentage cost-of-living increase were not made. Union contracts sometimes require such raises based on the Consumer Price Index and the Urban Workers' Family Budget figures, both of which are cited in determining the magnitude of the raises.

Wage Secrecy

Workers tend to decide on the equity of their pay by comparing it to that of the other workers. Employees seem to be able to find out each other's pay somehow. Thus, it is impossible for employees or employers to keep pay rates entirely secret. However, information on others' pay rates is often inaccurate, and thus misleading. Generally, employees think their pay is too low. They feel this way especially when they overestimate the pay of people below them and underestimate the pay of those above them. This creates dissatisfaction with pay due to the perceived inequities.

It is entirely proper for the foodservice organization to keep all pay rates secret. Good, open, and free communication among all of the staff is the only way to resolve feelings of dissatisfaction about pay. The use of evaluation techniques (see sections on Job Analysis in Chapter 5 and Evaluating Employees in Chapter 6) is sound management practice which assists in maintaining an equitable wage structure.

Equal Pay for Equal Work

In addition to the nondiscrimination implication of this principle, there is an implication of fairness and pay satisfaction if indeed equal pay is given for equal work. Well-constructed job analysis procedures are effective in ensuring equal pay for equal work. However, there are sometimes individual personalities present that make this principle less than perfect. There is a paramount need for the manager to adhere to the practice of tying pay rates directly to level of performance. Only in this way can each employee clearly recognize that the only way that his/her pay is going to be raised is for superior performance. The employee will see this as a very fair management practice.

Fringe benefits must be also related to performance. It is important to the employee to know exactly what these are and how substantial they become during the period of a year. Appreciating the magnitude and scope of fringe benefits helps to create in the worker the feeling that this foodservice really cares about its employees and is trying to do its best for the well being of all of the staff.

A COMPENSATION PLAN

The purpose of such a plan is to give employees a sense of fair treatment as to their pay and, at the same time, to control this very important cost of doing business. Pay is one of the key elements in increasing and maintaining productivity and morale. It also, of course, is a prime factor in attracting and keeping good employees.

Basic to a satisfactory employee compensation plan is that it will indeed attract the kind of people who are needed and thus be competitive with other similar organizations in the community. The plan must be viewed by members of the staff as fair and reasonable. Also, the plan must be managed in a completely objective and consistent way.

Management of the Compensation Plan

The main considerations in managing the pay plan is adherence to policies concerning:

1. Job evaluation (See section on this in Chapter 5.)
2. Individual employee performance appraisals (Review Chapter 6.)
3. Frequency and amounts of pay raises
4. Raises as related to promotions
5. Pay of new positions which might be created
6. Noncash compensations
7. Adherence to state and federal laws concerning compensation

Once the policies have been formulated, then the plan for carrying these out should be decided upon and consistently administered. All personnel must be treated alike. The Civil Rights Act of 1964 specifies that employees cannot be discriminated against regarding compensation, and the Equal Pay Act of 1963 states very clearly that there must be equal pay for equal work. There cannot be any pay differential based only upon the sex of the worker. Raises can, of course, be given for promotions, seniority, meritorious service or similar reasons.

Pay Ranges

Beginning or entry-level jobs for inexperienced people will probably be at the minimum wage level. However, obtaining good people at this level will depend on the supply situation. A shortage of applicants will tend to raise the amount of pay needed to attract satisfactory candidates.

A maximum pay might also be established for a particular job. However, if the cost of living continues to go up, maximum pay levels are likely to be raised. There would normally be a progression of pay increases from the minimum to the maximum. But at each stage or step a raise would be made if the employee stayed with the organization and reached the satisfactory skill levels.

If the foodservice is unionized, various levels of pay and agreements on pay ranges are usually spelled out in the contract. Cost-of-living adjustments might be included.

Pay Raise Policy

A variety of methods of giving raises can be used. Sometimes they are used together. For example, an employee might be awarded a merit raise and a cost-of-living raise together. However, cost-of-living raises as such are not recommended as a good pay policy. Better to give workers who have demonstrated good performance a sizable merit raise than to specify that this is a combination raise. Those with poor or unsatisfactory performance, as determined at the 6-month's evaluation meeting with their supervisors, would be given no raise. Each such person should be informed as to why the raise was not given, and what must be done to deserve a raise 6 months from now. If an employee in such a situation asks for assistance to achieve a satisfactory performance and to earn a raise, it is important to respond to this and provide the asked-for help. Sometimes slow starters end up as outstanding workers. Reviewing each employee's performance every 6 months is good personnel policy.

Ranking Method

By using job analysis, a series of job ladders can be created from beginner or apprentice to top-level performer. At each step in this ladder, a pay rate is decided upon. As the worker achieves experience, growing skill, and improved productivity, a promotion (possibly) and the next pay step is given. Encouragement to reach the next higher step, of course, would be good personnel practice.

If it happens that two jobs are very similar and it is difficult to really determine a clear-cut distinction, the use of "classes" can be helpful. For example, a class III baker would receive the same pay as a class III cook. There would be no further gradation of pay within the class III designation. The individuals involved know that they would have to be promoted to a class II cook or baker to receive a raise. The main idea here is to be sure that the employees know that better performance results in better pay and possibly a promotion which automatically means a raise in pay.

Financial Repercussions

Pay policies and the compensation plan have a most significant influence on profit levels. Budgets for wages and salaries are usually fixed in terms of a profit goal. Whether a raise is within the budget or not is the province of the controller or accountant. The financial consequences of awarding any raises must first be determined before any decisions are made. As a general rule, it is better to hire fewer people, work them harder and pay them more. This assumes that capable employees can be hired, trained, supervised and given incentive plans that bring about the level of productivity desired by management. Higher competency levels of such superior employees should bring about more sales. Thus, higher investments in good people should bring about higher returns.

FRINGE BENEFITS

Fringe benefits are an integral part of the compensation package today. The cost of these benefits can be as high as 35−45% of payroll.

In 1977 the Survey Research Center of the University of Michigan surveyed a large sample of workers and found that the most important fringe benefit was the hospital, surgical and health insurance coverage for illness or injury that occurs off the job. The survey asked workers the following question: "What fringe benefits which you receive are the most important to you?" The answers that they received were that the medical coverage previously mentioned was by far the most important.

The list of fringe benefits in order of their importance to the workers were as follows [adapted from Quinn and Staines (1977, p. 60)].

1. Medical, surgical, and hospital benefits (by far the most important)
2. Sick leave with pay
3. Retirement programs
4. Paid vacations
5. Life insurance, covering death unrelated to the job
6. Dental benefits
7. Profit sharing
8. Eye care benefits
9. Work clothing allowance
10. Skill training or education programs
11. Stock options
12. Free or discounted meals
13. Legal aid or services
14. Thrift or savings plans
15. Maternity leave with full reemployment rights
16. Free or discounted merchandise
17. Maternity leave with pay
18. Childcare services while parents are working

Subsequently it was further found that the average percentage of total payroll for indirect compensation has increased from 22.7% in 1955 to as much as 42% in 1980 and the yearly dollar amount has gone from $970 to approximately $5,500. At the present time the foremost fringe benefit is payment for Social Security—employer's contribution—which has shown a steady increase as a percentage for several years. One-half of the current percentage charge is deducted from the pay of the worker. The other half is contributed by the employer. Probably second in importance are the unemployment compensation benefits to which contributions are made totally by the employer. The rate here depends on the record of the company regarding laying off of employees. Considering medical and hospital benefits, the major public program is Medicare. This is now funded from the Social Security program. It applies only to those who are 65 or older. The Health Maintenance Act of 1973 is an attempt to provide medical and hospital benefits for younger people. The Act established Health Maintenance Organizations (HMOs) which incorporate the services of doctors, nurses, clinics and technicians. Patrons pay a single monthly rate. The Act requires employers of 25 or more people to offer an HMO option if they offer traditional health benefits.

There is no law that requires companies to provide private retirement benefits. Only about one-third of the entire U.S. work force is covered by private retirement plans. Most companies that have private retirement programs consider them to be noncontributory. The Employees' Retirement Income Security Act of 1974 was enacted to protect employees who were covered by private pension programs. If a company has or plans to have a private retirement program, it should comply with the minimum requirements of this Act.

Vacations with pay are also considered important fringe benefits. The average in the United States today is about 10 paid holidays off per year. The number of weeks of paid vacation varies but commonly these vary from 2 to 4 weeks per year on a national average.

Other types of fringe benefits can be considered, and probably the best plan is to discuss these matters with the employees. It is important to find out what their preferences may be. These will vary according to the economic circumstances of employees, their age, education and their vocational aspirations. Some prefer more days off for vacation while others might prefer some kinds of insurance coverage over other types. Older workers are more concerned about increased pension benefits. Employees with small children may prefer better hospital or dental benefits.

Benefits and Costs

One can calculate the cost of indirect compensation in several ways:

1. Total cost of these benefits annually for all employees
2. Percentage of payroll represented by the cost of indirect compensation
3. Cost per employee per year divided by the number of hours that this employee worked
4. Cost per employee per hour divided by the number of hours that the employee worked
5. Cost per cover served

Knowing these statistical facts relating to the indirect employee compensation program, one can calculate the benefits received from this in relation to the costs. Thus, one can determine the competitive situation with other foodservice organizations which may be competing for personnel.

Each year, such as the time when the W-2 forms are prepared, a summary of the total fringe benefits paid by the employer in behalf of each employee should be made. When this is transmitted to the employees it will impress on them the size and importance of their fringe benefits.

PROMOTION FROM WITHIN

Promotion from within is a standard practice in most organizations. Recruiting outside of the organization for a higher level position is often difficult. Promoting from within is a valuable guiding principle in recruitment. Selecting people initially who have the potential for promotion to higher positions should be preferred over those that appear to have little possibility of assuming increased future responsibilities. Educational training may very likely be required for anyone that is being promoted, however. (See section on Educational Upgrading in Chapter 6.)

Placing an employee in a trainee status or as an apprentice is a desirable policy. The person being upgraded or promoted is given adequate preparation for future additional responsibilities. Over the long pull, it is essential to be grooming particular individuals for increased future responsibilities. Any organization that relies entirely on one person for a key position is in a precarious situation. Consider what would happen if any one of your key people should suddenly depart your organization. Who would replace this person? Could the job then be adequately done?

RETIREMENT

People look at retirement in various ways. Some are very apprehensive about the removal of work from their lives. Others view retirement as an escape from the rigors of work and a time to pursue hobbies, travel, and self-improvement projects. For others, retirement is the start of a most exciting personal adventure into entirely new pursuits.

Employers share some of the responsibility of preparing employees for the day of retirement. Pre-retirement counseling and referral of the employee to social organizations that will provide future helps are some of the suggested procedures.

A company-paid retirement program was the third most important fringe benefit recognized by employees according to a study by the Survey Research Center of the University of Michigan in 1977. (The most important was medical and hospital insurance and the next in importance was sick leave with full pay.)

No private retirement programs are required by law. Pensions are most likely to be included in union contracts with firms employing over 500 workers. Most private plans are noncontributory, and thus, pay is less at retirement than government plans which require about 7% of the pay to be placed in a retirement fund. The Employees' Retirement Security Act (federal) was enacted to protect employees covered by private pension programs.

Insurance programs include life, health and disability. Often, these plans are continued by the employer after retirement. These constitute an important reward for the long-term employee and are greatly esteemed by them.

Some private plans provide for a certain amount of pension which they will receive upon achieving so-called vested rights. If the vested employee quits, he/she will receive some pension benefits. Those who are not vested who quit will receive no retirement benefits from that particular employer.

REFERENCES

CAUVIN, J.R.   1979.   The executive-compensation package: Salaries, bonuses, benefits, and perks. The Cornell Hotel and Restaurant Administration Quarterly *20*, 17–24.

FROST, C.F., WAKELEY, J.H., and RUH, R.A.   1974.   The Scanlon Plan for Organizational Development: Identity, Participation, and Equity. Michigan State Univ. Press, East Lansing, MI.

HILL, N., and STONE, W.C.   1977.   Success through a Positive Mental Attitude. Simon and Schuster, New York, NY.

LANE, H.E.   1976.   The Scanlon Plan: A key to productivity and payroll costs. The Cornell Hotel and Restaurant Administration Quarterly *17*, 76–80.

NEBEL, E.C.   1978.   Motivation, leadership, and employee performance: A review. The Cornell Hotel and Restaurant Administration Quarterly *19*, 62–69.

QUINN, R.P., and STAINES, G.L.   1977.   The 1977 Quality of Employment Survey. Survey Research Center, Univ. of Michigan, Ann Arbor, MI.

SIMMONS, J., and MARES, W.   1983.   Working Together. Alfred A. Knopf, New York, NY.

TOWNSEND, R.   1970.   Up the Organization. Alfred A. Knopf, New York, NY.

WALLACE, J.Y.   1984.   Foodservice wages must rise or living standards will fall. Restaurants and Institutions *94*, 79.

8 Avoiding Legal Problems and Losses

RESPECTING EMPLOYEE'S LAWS

"An ounce of prevention is worth a ton of cure" is a variation of the old saying, but it applies very well to the foodservice manager's responsibilities. Having a cooperative and competent legal advisor and/or C.P.A. is a first step in avoiding legal problems. In fact, a cadre of advisors—a banker, consultant, and insurance expert—is best. If it appears that a problem has legal ramifications, it is important to seek counsel. This is the only way to successfully stay out of legal trouble.

Each state and municipality has a collection of employment laws, some of which will apply to each business (Sherry 1982). There are also federal laws and these are listed here:

1. Old Age Survivor's Disability and Health Insurance (1935)
2. Unemployment Compensation (1935)
3. Worker's Compensation (dates differ state by state)
4. Fair Labor Standards Act (1938)
5. Equal Pay Act (1963)
6. Civil Rights Act (1964)
7. Age Discrimination in Employment Act (1967)
8. Occupational Safety and Health Act (1970)
9. Equal Employment Opportunity Act (1972)
10. Employee Retirement Income Security Act (1974)

11.   Pregnancy Discrimination Act (1978)
12.   Norris–LaGuardia Act (1932)
13.   National Labor Relations Act (Wagner Act) (1935)

Faithful adherence to all employee's laws is fundamental for any foodservice business. In such a labor-intensive operation, the smooth administration of these laws will do much to build harmony and good feelings between the management staff and the employees.

Legality of Employment Records

Although there is no specific federal law that applies to private employment record access by employees, several federal laws do affect private industry indirectly. Also, the various states may enact laws that are intended to protect individual privacy (McConnell 1982).

Basically what is intended by these laws is that employees should be entitled to inspect their personnel records from time to time. Also, the intention is that these records and the information contained in them should not be disclosed to third parties without notification to the employee. Thus, such laws influence the use of the personnel file, access to its contents, and the information that is usually collected and placed in the file. The attorney or C.P.A. should be consulted for recommendations as to handling of these files.

The following procedures are usually recommended:

1.   Each employee should have an individual employment file.
2.   The file should contain only a minimal amount of essential information.
3.   An employee has the right to inspect the file. However, there must be a written request to make this inspection. The manager will notify the employee of the time and place and this should be during working hours. A manager or supervisor should be present in the place where the inspection occurs. A reasonable time such as 30 minutes should be allowed. The employee may not remove any material from the file. Once per year is a reasonable frequency for such an inspection.
4.   Storage time requirements may vary by states. Expert advice should be obtained.

Affirmative Action Laws

It is important for a foodservice to make sure that its employment practices do not discriminate. However, it is also mandatory that management demonstrate that it employs minorities in proportion representative of their availability in the local area. Sex discrimination should be avoided by recruiting both sexes. Advertisements should avoid partiality for either sex. Pay, hours, and benefits must be equal for both sexes in specific job categories. There must be appropriate physical facilities for both sexes. Either sex must have access to jobs for which they are qualified. For females, child bearing must be considered a reasonable cause for a leave of absence. Seniority achievement may not be based on sex. No discrimination may be made on the basis of color, religion, or national origin.

Discrimination that bars women and minorities from higher level jobs is also illegal. Also, equal pay for equal work must be practiced in order to avoid prosecution. Pay of time and one-half for work over 40 hours is part of employment laws. In all of these legal matters, it is advisable to have an attorney to whom questions can be referred and who can give advice relating to employment laws (Stefanick 1981).

EMPLOYEE'S INSURANCE

There are three major types of employee's insurance programs: life, health and disability. If an organization provides these types of insurance coverages, they are usually provided far below the cost if paid by the employees buying their own insurance.

Life insurance programs are typically purchased to cover practically all employees. Benefits are commonly equal to 2 year's income, but this is more true for managerial employees than nonmanagerial. For nonmanagerial, the amount is often somewhat less than 1 year's income. At retirement, benefits continue for most employees but may be reduced by a particular percentage—something like two-thirds. Insurance programs are customarily noncontributory—the employee does not pay anything for this protection.

Regarding health insurance, usually the employee does not pay anything and the company pays the full cost. This coverage is provided to all employees. Managerial employees often have somewhat better coverage. A rather common provision is to have a deductible feature on their health insurance. Managers pay the first $50 or $100 before receiving the benefits of the insurance coverage. Nonmanagerial employees generally do not pay any deductible amount. Benefits that are provided by the health insurance program must be well defined by the organization, and each employee should have a complete explanation as to what these benefits are, what is covered, and the various features of the protection. Health insurance programs cover short-term absences from work due to sickness.

Long-term absences due to sickness or disability are covered by long-term sickness and disability insurance. These coverages generally take care of those losses not protected by federal disability programs. Thus, short-term disability protection is usually offered by smaller organizations, rather than offering long-term type of disability insurance. A smart idea is to make a summary at the end of each year of the value of the insurance coverage plus other "fringe" benefits received by the employee in terms of the total dollars that were expended for the employee's benefit. Most employees are not really aware of the value of these extra benefits—which actually are forms of indirect compensation. Typically, such indirect compensation may total as much as 45% of the total pay the employee received in the form of regular checks. So doing will impress upon the employee the value of these added indirect forms of compensation.

A local insurance broker can suggest appropriate coverages. Also, a C.P.A. firm can provide guidelines as to a reasonable level of cost of such employee protection.

The above descriptions are, of course, in addition to various kinds of employee insurance, required by law in the various states, such as worker's compensation and unemployment insurance.

THEFT PREVENTION AND SECURITY

Magnitude of the Problem

This is a difficult problem, a full discussion of which cannot be covered here. However, the essential elements will be presented. For full details, consult Axler (1974) and Curtis (1975).

Employee thefts are a serious problem and many millions of dollars in business losses from reported employee theft occur in the United States each year. Even more alarming, of the number of businesses that fail each year, the U.S. Department of Commerce reports that employee thefts were listed as the major cause of 34% of the cases. This is a very high failure rate. The National Restaurant Association estimates that five cents of every dollar in restaurant sales are lost to theft. Of that five cents, four cents are stolen by the employees. Most of the theft is in small items. But, these add up to big losses by year's end. Many owners and managers do not believe that their employees are stealing. But the above statistics indicate that stealing is indeed a most common occurrence. See also Coltman (1980) and Dittmer and Griffen (1979).

Another serious aspect of this problem is that thefts come out of net profits. A foodservice that makes a 3% net profit and has a 1% shortage has in fact lost 33.3% of its hard-earned profits. Employee thefts are a direct loss of profits to the business. Suppose a foodservice with $500,000 in sales found that it has a 1% shortage. It not only lost the $5,000 which is equivalent to the 1% shortage, but also lost all of the profits on the food that must be sold to pay for the shortage. The business would have to sell about $170,000 worth of food without any profit at all in order to pay for the $5,000 worth of food or money that was stolen. Thus, this foodservice would have to operate for several months each year just to pay for its losses through theft or embezzlement.

Employee theft has other undesirable effects. These include the loss of a once valuable employee found to be stealing, the expense of training a new replacement, the unwholesome influence on other employees who may start to steal because of the example, the lowering of employee morale, and even possibly bad publicity.

These are only part of the losses which can occur. Other merchandise thefts and losses include thefts by customers, supplier pilferage, and excessive losses through rough handling and damage to goods, thawing and damaged containers and contents.

Who Steals?

The worst offenders are believed to be hired managers and assistant managers—particularly the latter—and especially those in the kitchen and bar. Such employees are in the most favorable situations to steal, and thus, have more temptations than the more restricted employees. Their stealing may also be easier to cover up and may occur for long period of time. Thus, thefts by this group of employees can be the worst of them all. So, step one in preventing theft is to hire scrupulously honest managers, assistant managers and department heads. Careful employee screening, reference checking, and air-tight accounting, cash control, cost control and auditing procedures are some of the ways to obtain and keep honest managers. (Additional detailed suggestions to keep employees honest will be found subsequently in this section.)

Management—The Key

A program to reduce thievery and other needless losses must begin with the general manager. Unless this trustworthy manager really cares about the problem and is willing to work and think of every possible way to prevent theft, no amount of discussion or complaining will accomplish a thing. The manager must let every employee know how important it is to prevent thievery and losses. A vigorous training program for all old and new employees must be implemented. New employees, especially, must be trained to spot thefts or the opportunity for thefts and be rewarded in some way for

FIG. 1.   Employee's time clock is
clearly visible from main office.

bringing these situations to the attention of their supervisor or manager. It is
important to enlist the help of *all* of the staff if a well-planned procedure to
eliminate theft is to be successful. But the manager must make it very clear
to all that this is an *important* part of the business which deserves the
attention of all, especially the managers and the supervisors.

Suggested Policies

1.   Teach all employees that food, beverages, and condiments—anything edible as well as cleaning agents, linen and paper products—are the
same as money. They cost money and if they are wasted or stolen, it is
exactly equal to the amount of money that these cost. *Food = money.*

2.   Do not give away or sell food or beverage to employees. So doing
invites pilferage as these employees are tempted to "add a little" to the items
being taken home. It is all right to sell employees food, say at retail, and to
possibly give them a discount on the purchase price.

3.   Rules are made to be kept. Everyone including the manager, assistant manager, supervisors and owners must obey the same rules at all times.
No exceptions. The prevention system will not work if it is not adhered to
100%.

4.   Employee's cars must be parked as far from the workplace as possible and practical. Parking at an adjoining parcel of land or way in the back is
best. In planning a new business, employees should be required to walk past
a time clock (see Fig. 1) or office that is constantly occupied and to walk past
windows of the manager in order to reach the parking lot when leaving the
premises.

5. Require all employees to use one door only, whether coming or going. This applies to all—managers and owners—everyone working in the facility.

6. Check all parcels, packages, bundles, boxes, and similar objects carried by employees coming and going. A good practice is to issue parcel checks and keep such parcels in the checker's office to reissue to the owner upon departure. Audit this system regularly and do not allow presigned blank parcel checks.

7. Be extra careful in deciding who possesses keys. Only those who *must* have keys to storage areas are given those keys. They must be signed for and a record kept of who has what keys.

8. Doors to any type of storage areas must be kept locked at all times except when merchandise is going in or out (see Figs. 2 and 3). This is especially important at night when maintenance workers or employees working late or at unusual hours may be in the vicinity of the storage areas.

9. Rotate stock in storeroom prior to delivery. Use FIFO—first-in first-out principle of stock rotation. Whenever merchandise is received and checked, it should be stored in its proper place immediately. (See Figs. 4 and 5.) Failing to do so, invites thievery, thawing, deterioration and mechanical damage.

FIG. 2. Lock guards help to prevent thievery.

FIG. 3.   Deadbolt locks provide extra security.

10.   Check door alarms (see Fig. 6) on a regular schedule. If not done, chances are that in an emergency, the alarm will not sound. Months of pilferage may be taking place through a particular door if the alarm is as dead as the door material.

11.   Recognize that the inaction of the manager is often an integral part of the theft problem. Or the manager, assistant manager or a department head could be the problem.

12.   Control receiving documents by number to prevent fraud and duplicate payment. (See Fig. 7.)

13.   Occasionally make a deliberate error to test the operation of the receiving system.

14.   Require that scales be "zeroed" before checking weights of all shipments. (See Figs. 8 and 9.)

15.   Never allow employees, drivers or customers to pick and weigh their own orders.

16.   Check and supervise all waste and trash removal. Do not allow trash removal when it is dark outside. Sometimes the trash man is in collusion with someone in the kitchen. Good food or other items are placed in special bags and later divided up.

17. Be sure management is supplied with daily, weekly, monthly and quarterly reports of production, payroll and inventory levels. (See Figs. 10 and 11.)

18. Have managers and supervisors occasionally vary their time of arrival and departure from work.

19. Fire anyone caught stealing. Employees respect and admire a firm but fair boss. Swift punishment as an example does a lot of good.

20. Never allow the person who orders supplies to also receive these supplies. Collusion is one of the most common forms of theft.

21. Realize that according to good authority, 15% of any group of people will never steal. Another 15% will steal regardless of the security measures you take. The remaining 70% can go either way depending on the attitude of their managers, the controls which have been put in place, and what other employees seem to be able to get away with. In other words, it is possible that 85% of the employees could be stealing. This amazingly high percentage has been termed the "hustling mentality" wherein people see an

FIG. 4. Prompt removal of supplies ensures maintaining them in good condition.

FIG. 5.   As soon as possible, goods are placed in the proper storage areas to prevent loss and deterioration.

opportunity to get something for nothing. Many think this is the smart thing to do. Most pilfering involves what is thought to be small, insignificant items that are in good supply and will be missed by no one. Or "everyone is doing it so it must be all right." The victim of the theft is not even considered, and the thief does not recognize that stealing is morally wrong. Also, the employee may feel underpaid and steals in order to make up for the low level. Or "this is a big rich company and they will never miss this little item."

22.   If size of operation warrants, set up a security department or appoint a security officer. Good sources of such personnel are former or early retired police or FBI officers. Such people have had long experience in crime detection and prevention. Or hire a knowledgeable person as a consultant to create or improve the security system. A periodic review of the system is necessary in order to monitor its effectiveness.

23.   A recommended technique is to hire "shoppers" to observe how purchases and other transactions are being handled. They make reports on

FIG. 6. Door alarms should be tested weekly to be sure they are in proper working order.

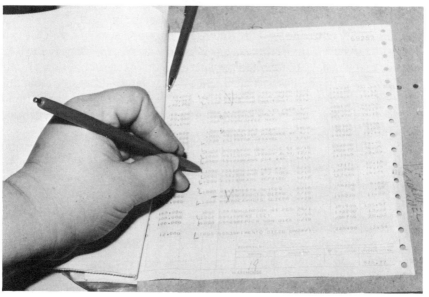

FIG. 7. Invoices are checked to be sure that all items ordered were received.

FIG. 8.   Scales are zeroed to ensure accurate weighing of incoming items.

their observations. Employees should be told that shoppers have been hired. This helps to prevent theft.

24.   To prevent theft by suppliers, send to each several copies of a "code of conduct policy statement." This statement lists the types of activities that will absolutely not be tolerated. Require each supplier to sign at least two copies of the statement, returning one copy to you. Another suggestion is to require that you have the right to conduct an audit of the supplier's accounts as related to your purchases. The practice of requiring bidding and competitive offers also helps to control shady practices. Even doing a background check on suppliers helps to reinforce faith and confidence in suppliers prior to making contracts.

25.   Insist on requiring that a copy of the purchase order accompany the delivery order. Any shortages or substitutions must be promptly reported to the persons most concerned. (See Fig. 12.)

26.   Use computerized registers. These provide a continuous inventory of merchandise. Any losses of products show up immediately and then the cause of the loss can be promptly investigated.

27.   Require that the manager or assistant manager personally supervise receiving all supplies delivered to the loading dock. By so doing, no opportunity for collusion or thievery can take place.

28.   Do not do office work at the same specific time each day. Vary your schedule, walking around the work areas at miscellaneous times during your

shift. If a manager develops the habit of working in the office at a regular time each day, someone tempted to steal will become aware of this and make plans for when the manager is not around.

Selecting Honest Employees

The first step in safeguarding a business from internal theft is to hire only honest people. However, this is not the easiest thing to do. When interviewing employees, look for the following traits:

1. A good positive attitude
2. Enthusiasm and interest in the job
3. Maturity and good judgement
4. Development of a real skill that is useful for the foodservice business
5. Tact and the ability to get along with other people
6. Integrity and a sense of moral and personal pride, conscientiousness and interest in job completion.

FIG. 9. A valuable meat item is weighed to verify that it is the correct amount.

FIG. 10.   Preparation of inventory levels is an important control procedure.

Checking References

People's characters do not change much after their basic personality develops at about 12 years of age. If they have been dishonest in the past they are probably going to continue to be dishonest. If an applicant has been convicted of some kind of property crime such as larceny, shoplifting, automobile theft, burglary, or robbery, it is not very likely this person will remain honest during employment. If released from prison after such convictions, he/she is not a very good bet from the security standpoint.

A manager should make sure to evaluate and check on all employment references that are provided by the applicant. The best way to do this is by telephone. It is important to discover if there were any instances of thievery in the applicant's previous employment. Another way to safeguard against hiring a dishonest person is to have the applicant fill out a bonding company application form along with the employment application. Most people with a criminal record will know that bonding companies often make an investigation into anyone who has filled out such an application and this is one way to weed out potentially dishonest employees. One can run a credit check through the bureau. Also, one can ask for the names of neighbors and

FIG. 11. Computerized equipment facilitates inventory control.

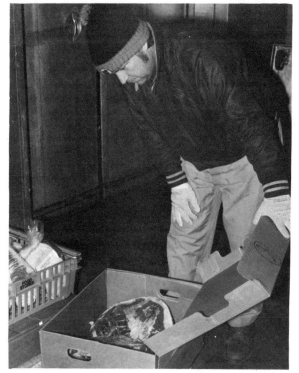

FIG. 12. Receiving clerk inspects meat shipment to verify its condition and that it is the correct cut.

friends and call some of them for information. "Crises" hiring should be avoided, if possible. Many applicants will falsify their credentials. If no background checks are made and they are hired, they have a low opinion of the employer as they were able to put one over on the organization. As soon as they become familiar with the foodservice's procedures, they begin to steal.

Suspicious Gestures

When interviewing prospective employees one should try to determine whether they appear to be overly nervous or whether they seem to evade questions which the interviewer would like to discuss with them. One should observe whether the applicant becomes excited or overly emphasizes any particular answers. Other gestures include rubbing the face or moving the hand across the face while talking, scratching various parts of the body or a sudden loss of color in the face. One can look for situations of excessive sweating or appearance of dryness of the lips or other nervous manifestations or gestures which indicate uneasiness on the part of the applicant.

When interviewing, one should be alert for indications of intelligence. An applicant who has graduated from high school should have at least a fair or average intelligence level. By discussing a candidate's preference in reading material one can sometimes judge intelligence level. However, any of these questions should relate directly to the job as much as possible. The questions formed might relate to reading material that has some relationship to the restaurant or food industry. It is important not to judge an applicant by what appears to be smooth slick behavior. Qualities of morality and integrity are very important. It is necessary to review the applicant's background. Revealing gestures might indicate overconcern about being asked certain questions.

Methods of Stealing

After being hired, the employee has to discover a method of stealing before the stealing takes place. The employee discovers some weakness in the foodservice controls system. Theft occurs by taking advantage of this weakness. An employee will try out a stealing method to see if it is discovered using only a small amount of goods or money. If it is not discovered then this becomes an avenue for much greater theft in the future. Employees also learn thievery methods from their associates. Employees even admire someone who has learned how to beat the system. When the manager learns how an employee steals, then it is much easier to prevent thievery. Some methods that are used follow:

1. *Switching guest checks.*　A waiter writes up guest checks for two tables of diners. The first one is the correct amount for the first table. He then makes up the guest check for the second table in the correct amount, but this table has a higher total check than the first table. The waiter then presents the check that was supposed to go to the second table and gives this to the first table. If the diners at this first table do not recognize that the check is too large, they pay the amount on the check. The waiter then substitutes the correct check which is a smaller amount and pockets the difference when he takes the money to the cashier. If the diners at the first table do recognize that the check is too large, they will object and then the waiter gives them the correct check and apologizes that he gave them the wrong check. If the waiter does receive too much money for the first check, he simply gives the correct check to the second table that he kept when he gave the correct first check to the cashier. So, no one is the wiser.

2. *Food going out the back door.*　Employees, especially chefs and cooks, can steal various types of food items by placing wrapped items in the garbage and then recovering them later. Or, they can throw the stolen goods out the back window where they are later recovered, or take the items out to their cars which are parked near the loading dock of the foodservice. They can give food to an associate or friend who drops by to see them or hide food items in their handbags or coats, large purses, or under their hats or some other concealment.

3. *Storage area thefts.*　Food can be stolen from storage areas especially during periods such as at nighttime when supervision is lacking. Food can be carried out in boxes and loaded into cars with very little difficulty.

4. *Kickbacks from vendors.*　This is a rather prevalent way of theft. Items are delivered in short quantity and if the receiving clerk is in collusion with the supplier the full amount of the shipment is acknowledged and subsequently paid for, but the amount actually received was short. The two parties then split the overpayment. A dishonest delivery person can raise the amount of the invoice in a number of ways and when the invoice is paid the two of them split the overpayment. Many other ways of shorting the foodservice by collusion between the vending company representative and the dishonest receiving clerk can be done.

5. *Embezzlement.*　Embezzlement is the dishonest appropriation of cash or checks which have been entrusted to the care of one of the employees. In this case, the two most vulnerable areas are the cashier's office and the accounting department where checks are disbursed. Forgery of checks is the most common form of embezzlement. Examples of how thefts can be made through embezzlement of checks are as follows: A clerk intercepts a check made payable to the foodservice. He then forges the company's name and cashes the check. Another method is to increase the face amount of the

check or change the name of the payee. A third way is paying an invoice twice and then appropriating the second check. Such thefts which are committed by bookkeepers or cashiers are usually serious because they are not discovered for quite a period of time. Another example would be a dishonest employee who sets up a nonexistent company and then prints up invoices from this nonexistent firm. The foodservice then pays these bills and the dishonest employee cashes the checks. Other methods are adding fictitious names to the payroll, cashing unclaimed wage checks, adding to expense accounts, making false income payments, and making false book-keeping entries. Cashiers can avoid ringing up sales and pocket the receipts, or ring up portions of sales. They can also give away meals or beverages or charge reduced prices. Another way that purchasing agents can embezzle is to be in collusion with various vendors. The invoices are "padded" by the vendor—stating prices higher than they are supposed to be. When the invoice is submitted for payment, the purchasing agent approves the payment. The amount of overcharge is split between the vendor and the purchasing agent. But instead of the agent receiving the money, the vendor or vendors pay a local business the amounts until a fairly substantial sum, such as $500 or $1000, has been accumulated. The store or auto dealer or whoever then notifies the purchasing agent that there is this amount credited to that person who should come in to make the selection.

6. *Cheating by linen suppliers.* Dishonest linen supply drivers can cheat the foodservice by placing part of the delivery of clean linens directly into the used linen containers. So doing increases the amount to be laundered or replaced and thus raises the cost to the foodservice.

7. *Stealing dishes, silver, napery, glasses, etc.* This is fairly common as these items are quite easily concealed. Strict indoctrination of new employees as to the need for complete honesty and ethical conduct is the best way to prevent thievery. Also, knowing that being fired is the sure consequence of getting caught is also a deterrent.

8. *Embezzlement by computer.* With the growing use of computers, knowledgeable persons can change the programming of the computer when no one is present. The output of the computer can be thus changed for their particular benefit. Since computers are becoming more sophisticated, it is also possible to increase substantially the amount of embezzlement that can be done through computer manipulation. Computer crime frequently involves collusion. To prevent this, it is necessary to restrict drastically the number of persons with access to both cash and the computer. These responsibilities should be divided. If it must be one person, it should be the owner or a wholly trusted manager. Ways to protect the business are to use transaction logs, which provide a trail that deters fraud, and to have a regular computer audit. The auditor will examine the performance of the

computer's accounting functions and verify answers on a separate computer. By this means unauthorized program changes can be discovered.

When Someone Is Caught

A structured procedure should be set up whenever an employee is caught stealing. This system should have a number of steps that are followed in investigating the case, trying to learn why it happened and how to prevent another one in the future. Why did the person steal? Who besides the thief was involved? What internal control problems should be corrected?

Following through on this systematic review, every case should be thoroughly analyzed. Any management people involved should be brought in to help make the investigation and develop the conclusions which will help prevent a similar incident in the future. For example, if it was a dishonest waiter, then the hostess or dining room manger should be involved and also the assistant manager in charge of that part of the foodservice. To complete the investigation, ask such questions as follow: Why was this particular person hired? What mistakes were made in selecting this individual? Was the thief's supervision adequate? Was the training adequate? Was the supervisor ever suspicious of this individual? If so, were the suspicions relayed to the manager? If not, why not? And, of course, in conclusion, what can the foodservice learn from this?

Once this investigation has been concluded, the foodservice's program of theft prevention will be substantially strengthened. Reduced occurrences of this type should thus be experienced in the future.

Stealing from the Bar

There are three main methods by which bartenders steal: (1) stealing bar receipts, (2) stealing liquor and (3) bringing in outside liquor to sell at the bar.

1. *Stealing money.* Receipts from bar sales are not rung up on the register. Or the price rung up is less than the actual price. The bartender pockets or places in the tip jar the difference between the amount paid and that rung up. When using these two methods, the money is sometimes left in the cash register until closing. Counting the cash in the register and totaling the reading on the cash register, the bartender then removes the amount of money representing the difference.

These practices can be eliminated by requiring written bar checks that are serially numbered and totaled each day. Also, the bartender should not be allowed to have access to the cash register readings at the end of the day. The new automated bar systems largely eliminate this problem.

2. *Stealing liquor.* Free drinks to customers is the most prevalent method. Also, the bartender will give free drinks to associates in the food-service in exchange for expensive food items such as lobsters and steak. Furthermore, the bartender can steal liquor by pouring it into some other type of bottle and taking this bottle home or giving it to someone else to remove. Fixing larger drinks than are specified by policy is another stealing practice.

The best way to avoid these problems is to use a computerized bar. It is important to establish firm policies. If the bartender does not comply with these policies after sufficient instruction and warnings, then he/she should be fired.

3. *Bringing in outside liquor to sell.* Bartenders can cheat by bringing in their own bottles. They then pour some drinks from these bottles and avoid ringing up the sale. So doing results in no discrepancy between the cash received at the cash register, the amount shown on the tape, and the inventory of the liquor.

Knowing what these methods are, management should be able to take vigorous steps to correct such dishonest practices. See also Albers (1974).

Storing

All liquor should be stored in a locked storage area and a key should be given only to those authorized to issue liquor. There should not be any extra keys in circulation. Whoever is in possession of a key should be responsible for the liquor.

Issuing

Issues from storage should be made only by written requisition. New shipments are added to the number of bottles in stock. Those issued to the bar should be subtracted. The balance or stock on hand should then be easily determined at any given time. This balance should be checked frequently (Bell 1976). Daily is best. An actual physical count is taken to be sure that all of the bottles are accounted for. Any shortages should be investigated immediately.

Employee's Rules and Regulations

No inventory or physical controls are as effective as good, honest employees who are very carefully selected, well trained and given competent supervision. Clearly defined sets of rules and penalties should be formulated. They should be applicable to all employees. Each employee must be taught to follow reasonable rules of conduct. If these are not followed, punishment should be the last resort when other methods have failed.

Everyone must be taught that it is important to work, cooperate, and behave in normal, friendly, and mutually helpful ways. They must be taught that it is important to report to work on time and when scheduled, perform a full day's work, respect the authority of their supervisor and manager, cooperate with fellow workers and behave in a reasonable and orderly manner. They must be expected to carry out job assignments promptly and capably. Most employees feel a need for job security. They wish to know that they are needed and that their cooperation is essential to the success that their organization deserves. Telling them this at appropriate occasions helps build morale and loyalty to the business.

Armed Robbery and Burglary

Foodservices, especially, are frequently targets for robbers. Those which sell for cash are more enticing than those with a large proportion of credit card sales. Also, many foodservices operate 24 hours per day or have a late closing hour. These increase vulnerability.

The best defenses against robberies are programs of top-notch employee training together with making the foodservice less appealing to robbers and burglars.

Each new employee is given specific instructions as to behavior during a robbery. Use of posters, film strips and teaching machines are effective. Such training is especially important for cashiers who should be instructed on how to deal with quick-change hustlers or grab-and-run thieves. Adequate training is also valuable to minimize violence that could involve customers. Courts will often hold a foodservice liable for violent acts such as shootings or injuries which occur on the premises.

Making the property less appealing to robbers requires the following procedures:

1. Limit the amount of cash in registers.
2. Use time-delay safes and change makers. However, this procedure has the possibility of violence. Post notices conspicuously that this is time-delay-type equipment.
3. Install a panic button or bar that sends an alarm to the police or alarm company.
4. Install a safe proximity alarm and backup system. The proximity device activates a noisy or silent alarm when someone comes near the safe. The noisy one has an advantage as it tends to scare away the thief and reduces property damage.
5. Have all employees leave the building at the same time. This avoids having a robber accosting the lone manager who is forced to reenter the

building and unlock the safe. Foodservices are the most vulnerable at opening and closing time.

6.   Contact local police officials for advice and cooperation in planning for burglary prevention. Use a police inspection notice at the main entrance. (See Fig. 13.)

7.   Provide ample outside lighting. This should be provided on all sides of the building, especially in the back. Keep lights on during periods of darkness.

8.   Do not deposit receipts in the bank at regular times. Vary these day by day so that a pattern is impossible for a potential burglar to detect.

Burglary Prevention

To prevent burglary the following questions should be asked:

1.   Are deadbolts needed? These are the most effective locks.

2.   Are all locks in good working order?

3.   Have all window locks been inspected for working condition? Have the window putty and general condition of windows been checked?

4.   Besides doors and windows, are there other means of building entry such as skylights or ventilators?

5.   Are door alarms or other types of alarms checked weekly?

6.   Has easily stolen equipment such as office machines and kitchen equipment been marked with engraving pens? (These pens are usually available at police stations.)

7.   Is there a decal on the front door stating that the premises is protected and patrolled by the police?

8.   Have all staff members been trained to be alert for any conditions that would facilitate a robbery?

FIG. 13.   Local police provided this warning decal for the restaurant's front door and also regularly inspect the premises.

9.   Is outside lighting adequate? (Lights should be recessed or otherwise protected to prevent destruction.)

10.   Is an inspection made each night before closing to be sure no one is in the building?

11.   Do all evening or night employees leave at the same time?

12.   Have burglary prevention methods been discussed with the police department and insurance representatives?

REFERENCES

ALBERS, C.H.   1974.   Food and Beverage Cost Planning and Control Procedures, Rev. Edition. Educational Institute, AHMA, East Lansing, MI.

AXLER, B.H.   1974.   Focus on Security for Hotels, Motels, and Restaurants. ITT Educational Publishing, Indianapolis, IN.

BELL, D.A.   1976.   The Spirits of Hospitality. The Educational Institute, AHMA, East Lansing, MI.

COLTMAN, M.M.   1980.   Cost Control for the Hospitality Industry. CBI Publishing Co., Boston, MA.

CURTIS, B.   1975.   Food Service Security, Internal Control. Lebhar-Friedman Books, New York, NY.

DITTMER, P.R. and GRIFFEN, G.G.   1979.   Principles of Food, Beverage, and Labor Cost Controls for Hotels and Restaurants, 2nd Edition. CBI Publishing Co., Boston, MA.

McCONNELL, J.P.   1982.   The laws of restaurants: Review and update. The Cornell Hotel and Restaurant Administration Quarterly 22, 25–29.

SHERRY, J.H.   1982.   The Laws of Innkeepers for Hotels, Restaurants, and Clubs. School of Hotel Administration, Cornell Univ., Ithaca, NY.

STEFANICK, G.J.   1981.   What you should know about the wage-hour law. The Cornell Hotel and Restaurant Administration Quarterly 22, 6–11.

Appendix A

Selected Job Descriptions

Bar and Beverage
    Bartender   148
    Bar Waiter/Waitress   149
    Wine Steward(ess)   150
Dining Room Service
    Bus Person (Bus Boy/Girl)   151
    Cafeteria or Grill Manager   152
    Catering Manager or Maître d'   153
    Dining Room Manager   155
    Food Checker (Cafeteria)   155
    Food Checker (Dining Room)   156
    Head Waiter   157
    Hostess/Host   158
    Steam-Table Attendant   159
    Waiter/Waitress   160
    Waiter/Waitress (Cafeteria)   162
    Waiter Captain   162
Food Preparation
    Baker   164
    Butcher   165
    Executive Chef   166
    First Cook   169
    Fry Cook   171
    Chef Garde-Manger   172
    Pastry Cook   173

Relief Cook	174
Second Cook	175
Short-Order Cook	176
Pantry Worker or Salad Maker	178
Vegetable Preparer or Cook Assistant	179
Kitchen Operation	
Dishwasher/Sanitation Assistant	180
Glass Washer	181
Kitchen Helper	182
Kitchen Steward or Steward	183
Tray Washer	184
Office and Building	
Bookkeeper	185
Purchasing Director	186
Receiving Clerk	187
Engineer	188

The following job descriptions have been adapted from the publication, "Job Descriptions in the Private Club Industry" published by the Club Managers Association of America, Bethesda, MD, in 1979. *Note*: These are illustrative examples and should be interpreted in light of the needs of a particular foodservice operation.

BAR AND BEVERAGE

Bartender

Job Summary

Stocks bar, mixes and serves alcoholic and other drinks, maintains bar in a clean, orderly condition, assists taking inventory of beverages and keeps department records.

Tasks Performed

1. Mixes and pours alcoholic and soft drinks to order, receiving payment or charge vouchers.
2. Maintains bar in neat, clean and attractive condition and keeps bar stock in prescribed manner.
3. Prepares and pours drinks to bar waiters/waitresses or to customers directly.
4. Stocks service bars and serves catered parties.
5. Washes glasses and other bar accessories and equipment.
6. Takes inventory and maintains records of drink popularity.
7. Reviews wine types and stocks popular brands and kinds.
8. Oversees cocktail lounge and supervises bar staff.
9. Prepares garnishes for mixed drinks and may premix drinks.

Equipment Used

Bung wrench; all types of liquor glasses; mixing spoons; paring knives; strainer; blender; muddler; jigger; ice picks; cutting board; cash register or computer terminal; account file; bar checks; cocktail shakers; automated bar

Material Used

Wines and liquors; beer, ales; mixes; soft drinks, juices, fruits; garnishes; ice; syrups, cream, milk

Relation to Other Jobs

Promotion from: Bar Helper, Cellarman, Bar Waiter, Assistant Bartender
Promotion to: Wine Steward, Head Bartender

Job Combination

Duties of this job may be combined with those of Wine Steward, Head Bartender.

Special Qualifications

Must be able (1) to mix all usual types of alcoholic beverages and know the proper procedures for handling and serving the various types of wines; (2) know portion control and methods for serving catered affairs; (3) be capable of operating the service bar without assistance; (4) keep accurate records of all sales at the bar and the control of cash and credit documents; and (5) be empathetic and, when time allows, listen sympathetically to customer's problems and give personal advice when asked.

Supervision[1]

Supervised by: Assistant/Food and Beverage Manager, Manager
Supervises: Bar Helper, Bar Waiters/Waitresses, Assistant Bartender

Bar Waiter/Waitress

Job Summary

Takes orders and serves customers, obtains check and sees that it is paid or signed, maintains cleanliness and order in serving area.

Tasks Performed

1. Politely asks patron for beverage order. Describes the types of cocktails, liquors, high-balls, and wines upon request.
2. Writes down the order on order book or pad.
3. Transmits order to Bartender; receives and places the order on tray and serves guests.
4. Receives check from Bartender and requests payment or credit information. Gives signed check or credit information to the Head Bartender or Tabulator.
5. Is responsible for obtaining appropriate payment, after being charged with an amount by, say, the Tabulator.

---

[1] In all of these job descriptions, the situation concerning supervision varies by foodservice. Shown are the most likely positions, combinations, and relationships. However, for any specific foodservice, the general manager determines the most advantageous supervisory organization.

6. Remains readily accessible and attentive to guests.
7. May dispense bottled beverages, soft drinks, juices, confections, tobacco, or serve any other item upon the request of the patron.
8. At catered parties, carries and serves drinks among the guests. If required, serves hors d'oeuvres and canapes to guests also.
9. When the guest leaves, cleans table with bussing towel and returns empty glasses to dishroom or appropriate area.

Relation to Other Jobs

Promotion from: Bar helper
Promotion to: Bartender

Job Combination

This job may be combined or included with that of the Bartender, Bus Boy or Waiter.

Special Qualifications

Must (1) possess knowledge of liquors and the ingredients used in making mixed drinks; (2) know the various types of wines and beers as well as the proper method of serving all drinks; and (3) must be hospitable, polite and gracious to customers and guests, making sales suggestions when appropriate.

Supervision

Supervised by: Bartender, Assistant Bartender
Supervises: Bar Helpers, Bus Boy/Bus Girl

Wine Steward(ess)

Job Summary

Supervises and trains Bartenders, Bar Boys and Waiters/Waitresses. Keeps controls necessary to minimize waste and theft. Requisitions additional supplies when needed and keeps necessary records.

Tasks Performed

1. Checks supplies of wines, liquors, mixing ingredients, glassware and other equipment.
2. Requisitions necessary replacements from Steward(ess), Purchasing Agent or Manager. May purchase supplies and beverages directly from suppliers.
3. Supervises and instructs Bartenders in the techniques of mixing and serving drinks. Sets standards and portions of beverages.
4. Sets up controls to minimize waste and theft.
5. Arranges for an adequate supply and efficient service of beverages for catered parties. Receives notification of special events from the manager and makes necessary provisions.
6. Employs, trains, discharges, and regulates hours of work and the wages of Bartenders, Bar Helpers and Bar Waiters/Waitresses.
7. Keeps revenue, time, inventory and production records.
8. May assist Bartenders to mix and serve drinks during rush periods.

Relation to Other Jobs

Promotion from: Head Bartender, Bartender, Cellarman
Promotion to: Purchasing Agent, Head Steward(ess)

Job Combination

The duties of this job may be included with those of the Cellarman, Head Bartender, Bartender, or Steward(ess).

Special Qualifications

Should be able to (1) mix all popular drinks and have considerable knowledge of standards, proportions, and price control; (2) recognize the various brands and types of wines and liquors, as well as proper storage procedures; and (3) determine work standards and schedules of Bar Waiters and other beverage employees.

Supervision

Supervised by: Purchasing Agent, Assistant/Food and Beverage Manager, Manager
Supervises: Bartender, Assistant Bartender

DINING ROOM SERVICE

Bus Person (Bus Boy/Girl)

Job Summary

Assists Waiters/Waitresses, maintains cleanliness and keeps dining room supplied with clean utensils, china, glassware, condiments and ice. Makes nonalcoholic beverages prepared in dining room.

Tasks Performed

1. Assists Waiters/Waitresses in their tasks.
2. Removes dirty dishes to the dish room.
3. Removes soiled linen and replaces with clean linen.
4. Replenishes butter supply.
5. Refills water glasses if necessary.
6. Brings clean silver to dining room station.
7. Sets up tables with silverware, glassware, and clean linen.
8. Is responsible for filling condiment containers.
9. May assist in carrying food trays to the table.
10. Makes coffee, iced tea, and fills ice boxes and bins.
11. Cleans and mops floors.
12. Dusts and cleans furniture, table tops; wipes chairs.
13. Helps wipe silver and glasses.
14. If required, may wait on customers and bring extra items to the patron.
15. Collects tips and places money in appropriate container or gives to designated individual.

Equipment Used

Trays or bins; wash cloths; broom; mop; carpet sweeper; cordless vacuum; dust pan; bucket; brush; uniform (usually furnished by employer)

Relation to Other Jobs

Promotion from: Dishwasher, Pot Washer
Promotion to: Bartender, Counter Helper in Snack Bar, Storeroom Helper, Sandwich Preparer, Waiter/Waitress, Cook Helper, Checker
Transfer from and to: Vegetable Preparer, Assistant Waiter, Bar Helper

Job Combination

The duties of this job may be combined with those of Dishwasher, Storeroom Clerk, Kitchen Helper, Kitchen Runner, Waiter/Waitress or Snack Bar Helper.

Special Qualifications

Must be able to (1) learn prescribed methods for removing dishes, setting tables and cleaning dining area; and (2) work rapidly during rush periods. Previous experience is not usually required.

Supervision

Supervised by: Bartender, Assistant Bartender, Waiters/Waitresses, Cooks, Cashier

Cafeteria or Grill Manager

Job Summary

Directs these informal dining areas. Supervises employees, orders supplies, helps plan the menu, and maintains payroll and bookkeeping records.

Tasks Performed

1. Manages the food areas where service is not formal.
2. Supervises the activities of Waiters, Countermen/Counterwomen, Bus Boys/Girls and other workers in the food areas, seeing that service to customers is prompt and courteous, adjusting complaints of customers, and coordinating the activities of the workers so that these food operations run smoothly and efficiently.
3. Plans menu in collaboration with the Chef, or Cook.
4. Orders food supplies (endeavoring to obtain the best quality at lowest possible cost); orders serving and cooking supplies and equipment.
5. Maintains payroll, time, and bookkeeping records; may serve as Cashier.

Relation to Other Jobs

Promotion from: Hostess, Cashier
Promotion to: General Manager, Assistant/Food and Beverage Manager

Job Breakdown

Purchasing of supplies may be done by Purchasing Agent.

Job Combination

Duties may be combined with Cashier or Hostess.

Special Qualifications

Must (1) be familiar with the fine art of service and (2) have the pleasure and enjoyment of the customer as the prevailing guideline of the dining room.

Supervision

Supervised by: Maître d', Assistant/Food and Beverage Manager, General Manager
Supervises: Captain, Waiters/Waitresses, Cashier, Bus Boys/Girls

Catering Manager or Maître d'

Job Summary

Supervises the serving of food, arranges banquets or parties, sells foodservice, and handles complaints; may be responsible for profitable operations of the Food Serving and Food Preparation Departments.

Tasks Performed

1. Supervises the daily service of food; inspects work of Head Waiters, Waiter Captains, Waiters, Waitresses, Bus Boys/Girls and other dining room employees; sees that service is technically correct, efficient and courteous; consults with Executive Chef, Steward or Chef—Steward concerning daily menus and operating problems; adjusts complaints concerning service or quality of food; acts as contact between the Food Serving Department and the customers.
2. Makes arrangements with guests, in person or by letter, for banquets, special luncheons, and other social affairs; obtains pertinent information from the special catering sales representative or convention sales manager as to the number of persons expected, seating arrangements, decorations, music, and entertainment desired; analyzes the requirements of any special occasion and informs the group representative of suitable types of service; decides upon and quotes prices, attempts to sell the various services of the foodservice; draws up the contract and procures the group representative's signature.
3. Transmits necessary information to Chef, Head Waiter, Steward, and other employees concerned; arranges for such details as the printing of menus, procurement of decorations and entertainment, table setup, and the foodservice schedule; arranges for publicity if desired.
4. Inspects finished arrangements; may be present at time of banquet, supervising service and greeting guests.

The duties performed by a Catering Manager, Executive Chef, or Steward depend in great measure upon the size and organization of the foodservice, the policy of the management, and upon the individual worker's ability. In large establishments, especially in the southwestern parts of the country, the Catering Manager may have complete charge of food preparation, foodservice, beverage service, and banquet service. In such a case, he/she would make up and assign prices to items on menus, keep cost accounts, and assume responsibility for making a net profit out of food preparation and service. Under such circumstances, the worker might be titled "Food Manager." The Food Manager would either supervise and coordinate the work of a Banquet Manager, Chef, Steward, Maître d' (who would be directly responsible for foodservice only) and a Social Director, or he/she might perform some of the tasks of any or all of these workers.

The Social Director would have charge of social affairs, caring for guests' comfort and amusement and arranging and promoting social functions such as luncheons, dinners and parties.

The Banquet Manager would arrange the details of banquets, providing the necessary physical equipment and employing additional workers. During the banquet, he/she would act as Head Waiter supervising the service of food to make sure that it is correct, on time and as ordered.

Relation to Other Jobs

Promotion from: Head Waiter, Purchasing Agent, Chef, Steward
Promotion to: Manager

Job Combination

The duties of this job may be combined with those of the Head Waiter, Steward, Banquet Manager, Wine Steward, Social Director, or Purchasing Agent, or they may be included in those of Manager.

Special Qualifications

(1) May need to graduate from a hotel school. (2) Could have experience as Catering Manager in a hotel. (3) May need European training. (4) Must have ability to meet the public and to sell foodservices, a practical knowledge of food preparation and purchasing, a knowledge of social customs and etiquette (especially in regard to banquets) and a knowledge of wines and liquors.

Special Considerations[2]

How many employees are supervised and what are their titles? Does worker assume responsibility for food preparation as well as service? What type of dining rooms are supervised? Does worker supervise beverage department?

Supervision

Supervised by: General Manager
Supervises: Head Waiters, Waiter Captains, Waiters/Waitresses, Bus Boys/Girls

---

[2] The answers to the question(s) in this section can be incorporated into the preceding job description, along with any necessary adjustments or additions, to tailor it to the operation.

Dining Room Manager

Job Summary

Directs all services of the dining room. Supervises employees, orders supplies, helps plan menu, and maintains payroll and bookkeeping records.

Tasks Performed

1. Is in charge of dining areas and may also be in charge of informal areas such as grill and cafeteria. Supervises foodservice employees in accordance with operating policies which he/ she may help to set up.
2. Responsible for maintaining records or personnel performance and dining room costs.
3. Inspects foodservice personnel as to their appearance.
4. Checks special function sheets against room setup and personnel scheduled. May work with Maître d' or Catering Manager in scheduling functions.
5. Schedules periodic foodservice employee meetings to ensure correct procedures of food and beverage service and provides current instructions.
6. Trains Head Waiters, Captains and Staff to handle the various types of foodservice.
7. Handles complaints of customers.
8. Executes the general responsibilities necessary to help minimize the costs of operating the foodservice.
9. Assists in the planning of menus with the Maître d' or Executive Chef for special parties.
10. Schedules employees for each dining room.
11. Establishes standards of performance such as the amount of linen to be used in dining areas, number of covers to be served per employee and labor cost goals.

Relation to Other Jobs

Promotion from: Captain, Waiter/Waitress, Dining Room Cashier
Promotion to: Maître d', Assistant Manager

Job Combination

The duties of this job may be combined with those of Maître d', Captain, and Dining Room Cashier.

Special Qualifications

(1) Must be thoroughly familiar with the organizational procedures of the foodservice. (2) Must know proper methods of food and beverage service, food and beverage costs, and etiquette and social customs of banquet and party functions.

Supervision

Supervised by: Catering Manager, Assistant/Food and Beverage Manager
Supervises: Hostess, Maître d', Waiters/Waitresses, Bus Boys/Girls

Food Checker (Cafeteria)

Job Summary

Totals orders on customers' trays; assists wherever possible.

Tasks Performed

1. Makes rapid and accurate itemizing and totaling of orders on customers' trays.
2. Prepares menu boards.
3. Assists other workers with various simple tasks such as placing price markers on foods, refilling condiment containers, and taking inventory of dishes and silverware.
4. May act as Cashier or Hostess/Host.

Equipment Used

Checking machine, cash register, menu boards, and general office supplies used in cafeterias, such as rolls of paper for checking machine, report forms and record sheets

Relation to Other Jobs

Promotion from: Pantryman or Pantrywoman, Counterman or Counterwoman, Steamtable Attendant.

Promotion to: Hostess, Cafeteria Assistant Manager, Cashier, if the duties of Food Checker (Cafeteria) include none of the duties of Cashier

Transfer from and to: Cashier, Food Tabulator (Cafeteria), Counterman or Counterwoman, or Hostess

Job Combination

The duties of this job may be combined with Cashier or Cafeteria Assistant Manager.

Special Qualifications

(1) Ability to quickly memorize numerous food prices. (2) Imperturbability, an important quality.

Supervision

Supervised by: Hostess/Host, Dining Room Manager, Assistant/Food and Beverage Manager

Food Checker (Dining Room)

Job Summary

Checks food quality and quantity, and tabulates the price of each individual order or portion of food; may act as Cashier.

Tasks Performed

1. Checks orders: Scans trays to make sure that all orders contain the specified portions and that the quantity and quality of portions being served conform with predetermined standards set by management.
2. Tabulates bills: Inserts check in register or calculator; itemizes food by touching the number keys; obtains total; removes check from register and places it on tray. In some establishments, tabulating machines are not used and in these instances the worker performs the same work but tabulates and adds the items on a check using a pencil.

3. Checks silverware used in service to areas outside of dining room. Makes an itemized list of silverware contained on tray being sent out of dining room; retains list, checking it against returned silver to decrease the possibility of loss through theft.
4. Compiles, tabulates and prepares a complete audit of portions of food served; at the end of each meal period summarizes all sales; prepares and submits report to Cashier to enable a balance to be made against cash receipts and charge accounts.

Equipment Used

Checking machine, cash register, computerized equipment, and general office supplies, such as record sheets, sales checks, inventory sheets, report forms, or special software

Relation to Other Jobs

Promotion from: Pantry Worker, Waiter, Waitress (Informal), Bus Boy/Girl, Coffee Preparer, Counterman/Counterwoman, Steam-Table Attendant, Pantry Supervisor
Promotion to: Steward, Assistant Manager, Cashier

Job Combination

The duties of this job can be combined with those of Cashier (Dining Room) or Assistant Manager.

Special Qualifications

Should be (1) skilled in critically examining foods on plates to detect improperly cooked foods by appearance or taste; check orders; (2) able to tabulate and add items rapidly.

Supervision

Supervised by: Catering Manager, Hostess, Dining Room Manager, Assistant/Food and Beverage Manager

Head Waiter

Job Summary

Assigns customers or guests to tables about dining room in such a way as to utilize staff and table space to best advantage or to give the appearance of a well-filled establishment; oversees activity of Captains, Waiters, and other dining room employees to ensure maximum service to customers.

Tasks Performed

1. Inspects dining room and employees; observes appearance of employees, paying particular attention to their dress and cleanliness; looks over dining room and equipment to make sure that everything is clean and properly arranged; gives orders to subordinates for any changes.
2. Greets customers entering dining room; asks how many are in party, and suggests a table; calls Waiter Captain and tells him where to seat guests; may escort them to table if Waiter Captain is not available; assists patrons to be seated and hands each one a menu; calls Waiter (Formal) to take order; may take order personally if guests so request and

give it to Waiter afterward; receives and adjusts complaints as to food or service; approves all exchanges as to food or service; approves all exchanges or returns of food; speaks to all departing customers or guests, calling them by name if possible and inviting them to return.
3. Calls Waiters' and Waiter Captains' attention to mistakes they may have made; offers suggestions and gives orders to correct such mistakes. (The Head Waiter never reprimands his subordinates in front of the guests.)
4. Holds periodic meetings as often as needed with the dining room employees for the purpose of discussing various aspects of service and causes of complaints.
5. Employs and discharges dining room employees; instructs, supervises, and assigns stations to them, rotating Waiters/Waitresses so that each has an equitable service load.
6. Maintains time record cards of employees; makes out employees' payroll; issues pay envelopes to employees; grants sick leave and time off to employees; makes a written report of all accidents or damages to persons or property occurring in the dining room.

Equipment Used

Tuxedo or dark suit usually furnished by employee

Relation to Other Jobs

Promotion from: Waiter Captain, Waiter/Waitress (Formal or Informal)
Promotion to: Catering Manager, Steward

Job Combination

The duties of this job may be combined with those of Waiter (Formal), Banquet Manager or Waiter Captain, or included in those of Catering Manager.

Special Qualifications

(1) Must fully understand the operation of dining room, proper service to be used for all occasions, and the duties of all subordinate employees. (2) Knowledge of etiquette must be up to date and complete.

Special Consideration (See footnote 2, p. 154.)

Does worker perform the tasks of a Banquet Manager?

Supervision

Supervised by: Maître d', Catering Manager, Dining Room Manager, Assistant/Food and Beverage Manager
Supervises: Waiters/Waitresses, Bus Boys/Girls, Cashier

Hostess/Host

Job Summary

Receives and seats guests, supervises dining room employees, maintains order and cleanliness, adjusts complaints, may keep employees' time records.

Tasks Performed

1. Greets guests entering dining room and escorts them to table; opens menu and places it on table in front of guest.
2. Supervises and instructs Waitresses and Bus Boys/Girls.
3. Inspects the dining room; directs Waitress or Bus Boys/Girls to change the table linen or to set the table when necessary.
4. Reserves tables upon request.
5. May employ and discharge Waitresses and Bus Boys/Girls.
6. May receive and adjust complaints concerning food or service.
7. Maintains time records of employees.
8. May check quality and quantity of food and beverages served.

Relation to Other Jobs

Promotion from: Food Checker (Cafeteria), Counterman/Counterwoman, Waiter/Waitress (Informal), Cashier, Food Tabulator (Cafeteria), Pantryworker

Job Combination

The duties of this job may be combined with those of Waiter or Waitress (Informal), Food Checker (Cafeteria), Food Tabulator (Cafeteria) or Manager Assistant (Dining Room), or included in those of Cashier under the title Cashier Hostess/Host.

Special Qualifications

(1) Must present a neat attractive appearance; (2) possess a well-modulated speaking voice and an outgoing pleasant personality. (3) Should have tact, good judgment and politeness—especially important characteristics. (4) Must know the proper method of setting a table for all occasions.

Special Consideration (See footnote 2, p. 154.)

Can worker perform clerical duties such as keeping time records?

Supervision

Supervised by: Dining Room Manager, Assistant/Food and Beverage Manager
Supervises: Waiters/Waitresses, Food Checker, Food Tabulator, Bus Boys/Girls, Cashier

Steam-Table Attendant

Job Summary

Serves hot foods to Waiters/Waitresses and customers from steam table.

Tasks Performed

1. Wipes dust from steam-table frame, shelves, food containers, glass counters and serving equipment with damp cloth; lights gas jets or turns valve to adjust steam, and places water in the steam-table eyes (recessed compartments).

2. Obtains or receives containers of food and serving accessories; places these items in and on steam tables so that the more popular foods are most accessible and those requiring most heat are located in the warmest part of the table.
3. Carves and serves meats; portions vegetables and other prepared food to order so that each plate presents a neat, appetizing appearance.
4. Obtains or requests additional supplies to replenish steam table when necessary.
5. Clears steam table. Removes containers of food, turns off gas, empties water from eyes by opening exhaust valves; washes, scours and polishes table using soap, water, metal polish, brushes and cloth.
6. May prepare and serve beverages and various kinds of salad dressings.

(Slicing meats, which requires the ability to work accurately at a rapid pace for short periods of time, makes the greatest demands of this worker.)

Equipment Used

Steam table, carving equipment, such as knives and forks; serving equipment, such as ladles, scoops, metal containers, bowls, soup tureens, chinaware, and silverware

Working Conditions

Surroundings: Inside, sometimes hot and humid

Relation to Other Jobs

Promotion from: Sandwich Preparer, Bus Boy/Girl
Promotion to: Cook, Counter Supervisor, Counterman/Counterwoman, Food Checker (Dining Room or Cafeteria)
Transfer from and to: Waiter/Waitress

Job Combination

Could be combined with Cashier, Cook, Apprentice Cook, or Kitchen Helper.

Special Qualifications

Must (1) work rapidly during meal serving times, (2) pay attention to numerous details, and (3) be gracious to patrons. (4) Must have good hearing to understand orders.

Supervision

Supervised by: Dining Room Manager, Assistant/Food and Beverage Manager

Waiter/Waitress

Job Summary

Sets tables and serves meals to customers and guests according to well-established rules of etiquette, and performs various incidental duties to furnish satisfactory service.

Tasks Performed

1. Reports to Head Waiter or Hostess/Host to receive instructions about the menu and to

obtain checks for writing orders; familiarizes self with menu, paying particular attention to "specials."

2. Sets assigned tables: Spreads clean linen and places glasses, condiment holders, flowers, and silverware on table.

3. Receives guests and takes order: Assists Head Waiter or Hostess/Host to seat guests by pulling chairs away from table; distributes menus and fills glasses with ice water while guests decide upon order; writes order on check; answers questions about the food and menu and may make suggestions about various dishes and wines.

4. Tells Cooks of order; assembles food on tray, procuring items from each station or from a central serving counter; carries tray to the Food Checker who prices items listed on check.

5. Serves meal: Places tray on a stand near the table being served; places dishes, by courses, in front of each person, serving from the left of the patron; replenishes water and butter if needed, or requests Bus Boy/Girl to perform this duty. An efficient worker places dishes in front of each guest in such a manner that the guest can start to eat immediately upon being served.

6. Removes soiled dishes or requests Bus Boy/Girl to do so; procures and serves dessert; may place finger bowls in front of each guest.

7. Gives check to guests when they have finished eating, and either receives immediate payment (in which case it is taken to Cashier), or permits customers or guests to sign credit documents.

(This job makes numerous exacting demands upon the worker. A meal may consist of up to seven courses and may be accompanied by various wines. The worker must know how to regulate service so that each course will immediately follow the one preceding it, so that guests do not feel a lack of attention. To perform this job competently, the worker must know the types of wines that accompany a meal and how long it takes to complete any course on the menu and must be able to intelligently plan for, and regulate the service of, numerous different meals when serving several groups simultaneously.)

Relation to Other Jobs

Promotion from: Head Bus Boy/Girl, Bus Boy/Girl, or Bar Boy
Promotion to: Waiter Captain, Head Waiter

Job Combination

The duties of this job may be included with those of Head Waiter, Waiter Captain, or may be combined with those of Bus Boy/Girl, Cafeteria Manager, Cashier, Coffee Preparer, or Head Bus Boy/Girl.

Special Qualifications

(1) Must be thoroughly familiar with American and foreign dishes and all types of alcoholic beverages. (2) Must know how to pronounce the names of foreign preparations and what beverages to serve with them. (3) Must know proper meal serving techniques. (4) Should be anxious to please and have a genuine desire to serve and aid others.

Supervision

Supervised by: Captain, Head Waiter, Hostess, Maître d', Dining Room Manager, Assistant/Food and Beverage Manager
Supervises: Bus Boys/Girls

Waiter/Waitress (Cafeteria)

Job Summary

Helps customers with trays; removes dishes in a quick and efficient manner. Keeps dining area supplied with condiments and in a clean, orderly condition.

Tasks Performed

1. Sets up cafeteria and grill tables by placing linen, sugar bowl, and condiment containers on them.
2. Scrubs tables and cleans chairs; collects empty trays and carries them to the kitchen; may remove dirty dishes from tables and carry them to Dishwashers.
3. May take customer's order for additional food, get food from counter and carry it to patron, collecting amount due and turning money over to Cashier or having customer sign a charge form.
4. May carry filled trays from counters to tables for customers.
5. May serve ice water, coffee, and bread or biscuits to patrons at tables.

Equipment Used

Wash cloths, cleaning cloths, uniform (which may be furnished by employee), trays

Relation to Other Jobs

Promotion from: Coffee Preparer (Cafeteria)
Promotion to: Counterman or Counterwoman, Steam-Table Attendant, Food Checker (Dining Room), Food Tabulator (Cafeteria)

Job Breakdown

Parts of this job may be performed separately by a Coffee Preparer.

Job Combination

The duties of this job may be combined with those of Counter Attendant.

Special Qualifications

This is a beginning job for which experience is not usually required.

Supervision

Supervised by: Cafeteria Manager
Supervises: Bus Boys/Girls

Waiter Captain

Job Summary

Under general supervision of Head Waiter, has charge of one section of dining room, supervising, instructing, and assisting Waiters and Bus Boys/Girls; receives guests and conducts them to tables; may, upon request, describe or suggest various dishes and the wines that accompany them.

Tasks Performed

1. Escorts guests to tables (or see item 2).
2. Receives customers and guests after their greeting by the Head Waiter, who states the number of people in the party, and conducts them to their table of appropriate size.
3. May ask guests about their preference of location and strive to accommodate them; endeavors to seat patrons so that each Waiter will have an equitable service load and the more efficient Waiters will be able to serve more patrons.
4. Helps customers and guests to be seated and distributes menus; signals Bus Boy/Girl to fill water glasses and procure butter; returns to table upon request and either writes order on check or makes mental notes of it.
5. May, upon request, describe or suggest various dishes and the wines that may accompany them; determines the amount of service needed to efficiently serve the meal; assigns the necessary Waiters and Bus Boys/Girls, transmitting the order to them; withdraws to receive next guest.
6. Watches all tables under his supervision to detect any dissatisfaction, annoyance, slow or incomplete service, and makes the necessary adjustments.
7. Receives complaints or refers them directly to the Head Waiter.
8. May make written or verbal reports of accidents to Head Waiter for discussion in weekly staff meetings to improve future service.
9. May assist Waiters to reset tables and serve large parties during rush hours; may serve special parties upon request.
10. May prepare certain dishes at tables, especially flamed items.

Relation to Other Jobs

Promotion from: Waiter (Formal)
Promotion to: Head Waiter

Job Combination

The duties of this job may be included with those of Head Waiter, or may be combined with those of Waiter (Formal).

Special Qualifications

(1) Must be thoroughly familiar with both American and foreign dishes and the various beverages that may accompany them. (2) Must understand proper service to use for all occasions and possess a complete and up-to-date knowledge of etiquette.

Special Considerations (See footnote 2, p. 154.)

How many employees does worker supervise? Is dining room service formal, semiformal, or informal? Does worker adjust complaints?

Supervision

Supervised by: Head Waiter, Dining Room Manager, Assistant/Food and Beverage Manager
Supervises: Waiters/Waitresses, Bus Boys/Girls

FOOD PREPARATION

Baker

Job Summary

Bakes bread, rolls, muffins, and biscuits for consumption in dining rooms; mixes ingredients to make the dough; and cuts and shapes dough by hand or machine.

Tasks Performed

1. Studies current and next day's requirements.
2. Plans production in order to have bread, rolls, biscuits, and muffins freshly baked when needed and in quantities specified.

(In establishments where there is no Pastry Chef, the Baker may make and bake or have charge of the baking of pies, cakes and pastries. In many establishments the work of the Baker is shared by a Baker Assistant who kneads and shapes dough and usually mixes and bakes dough for simpler breads. In large establishments the work of the Baker may be performed by a Benchman who kneads, cuts, and shapes dough preparatory to baking; an Ovenman who bakes the dough; a Night Baker who mixes dough for the following day's baking and in many cases shapes it as well; and a Head Baker who plans production and supervises and assists the other workers.)

Working Conditions

Surroundings: Inside; usually hot
Hazards: Minor burns from oven or hot pans

Relation to Other Jobs

Promotion from: Baker Assistant, Ovenman, Benchman, Night Baker
Promotion to: Pastry Chef
Transfer from and to: Pie Maker

Job Breakdown

The duties of this job may be divided between the Baker and Baker Assistant, Benchman, Ovenman, Night Baker, and Head Baker; or Rolls Baker, Bread Baker, and Biscuit Baker.

Job Combination

The duties of this job may be combined with those of Baker Helper, Pie Maker, Dessert Cook, or Pastry Cook; or they may be included with those of Pastry Chef or Chef.

Special Qualifications

(1) Must be able to make all kinds of bread. (2) Should be able to bake previously prepared pastries and to make special types of breads (such as cornbread). (3) May be required to make Danish pastries.

Special Physical Requirements

Strength to lift heavy bags of flour, weighing as much as 100 pounds. Keen sense of taste and smell to determine whether ingredients are properly seasoned and sufficiently baked.

Special Considerations (See footnote 2, p. 154.)

Is worker expected to furnish own recipes, or must those of the foodservice be used? What is size and type of oven (electric, gas, or steam)? How is mechanical equipment operated? What average production is required? How many types of breads and rolls are baked? Are pastries or pie shells baked by worker? Is worker required to furnish own uniform?

Supervision

Supervised by: Chef, Sous Chef, Assistant/Food and Beverage Manager
Supervises: Baker Assistant

Butcher

Job Summary

Cuts, trims, and prepares meats for frying, roasting, broiling and stewing to order of various Cooks; makes individual cuts of meat to a specified size or weight and in such a manner as to utilize every portion of the carcass; stores supply of meats in the proper refrigerated equipment.

Tasks Performed

1. Receives notification from Chef or Cooks of meats to be served, and obtains meats needed from Steward, Storeroom Clerk or Purchasing Agent.
2. Weighs and inspects incoming meats and stores them in refrigerators or freezers, hanging quarters and large cuts on hooks, placing small cuts on shelves or racks. Lamb and veal may be received as whole carcasses and then split in half and quartered with a cleaver or bandsaw. Beef and pork are usually received quartered, or in smaller packinghouse cuts. (All cutting is performed on a cutting block.)
3. Cuts, trims, bones, and shapes beef, pork, veal, and lamb to make such cuts as steaks, chops, roasts, and cutlets; uses knives, cleavers, and a hand or electric bone or meat saw to cut meat, bones, and trim off fat and gristle. Cuts meat away from bones with boning knife; uses a steel needle and cord to sew meat together and pins (skewers) to hold and shape meat cuts like roasts; pounds meat with a mallet, side of cleaver or flattener to soften and shape it. Cuts steaks, chops and cutlets into portions that will be served to customers. (Roasts and meats that will be baked are carved and portioned by the individual who cooks them.) Cuts meat to the size or weight management has predetermined and utilizes every portion of each carcass in some manner.
4. Chops up or grinds meat for sausages, hamburger, stews, and soup stocks.
5. Slices meats like ham and bacon using a knife or meat slicer.
6. May pickle beef or other meats in a brine solution to make products such as corned beef.
7. Places prepared meats in refrigerator, from which they are issued to Cooks; may weigh cuts of meat before their issuance.
8. Renders fat.
9. Keeps records of meats received and issued, fat, bones, and other leftovers disposed of.
10. Assumes responsibility for the cleanliness of refrigerators, freezers, chopping blocks, tools and other equipment; may scrape, scour and clean them (usually done by an Apprentice or Helper).
11. Usually supervises an Apprentice or Helper.

(Utilizing, every portion of a carcass, without waste, and cutting meats into uniform portions of a predetermined weight or size, requires much skill. Job is now less common due to preportioned meats and poultry.)

Equipment Used

Refrigerator, freezer, cutting block, knives (cutting and boning), cleavers, bone or meat saws (hand or machine), scales, slicing machine, cutter, grinder, needles, cord, skewers, mallet, flattener, steel, hone, steam kettle, clerical supplies, white hat, jacket and apron

Working Conditions

Surroundings: Cold in refrigerator; workroom may be hot if butcher shop is near cooking ranges.
Hazards: Cuts from knives, cleaver, saw, grinder, or bones in meat; falling on wet floor of refrigerator

Relation to Other Jobs

Promotion from: Chicken and Fish Butcher, Butcher Helper
Promotion to: Garde-Manger, Garde-Manger Assistant

Job Breakdown

The duties of this job may be divided between a Butcher (Cold Cuts) and a Butcher (Fresh Cuts), or a Meat Butcher and a Butcher Assistant.

Job Combination

The duties of this job may be combined with those of Broiler Cook, Chicken and Fish Butcher; Butcher Helper or Garde-Manger Assistant; or they may be included in those of Chef, Fry Cook, Roast Cook, Garde-Manger, or Second Cook.

Special Qualifications

(1) Must know how to cut meats exactly for the proper cooking and type of service; (2) must be able to cut meats to a predetermined size or weight and in an efficient manner to eliminate waste. (3) Must be strong enough to lift heavy pieces of meat.

Supervision

Supervised by: Chef, Sous Chef, Assistant/Food and Beverage Manager
Supervises: Butcher Assistant

Executive Chef

Job Summary

Manages the kitchen and is responsible for all food and some types of beverage production. Plans menus in cooperation with Food and Beverage Manager, Assistant Food and Beverage Manager, Catering Manager and Convention Sales Manager. Supervises all kitchen employees. Monitors food cost ratios to ensure profitability or compliance with desired relationships. See Table 1.

Tasks Performed

1. Plans all menus including special parties and catering functions. Particularly evaluates popularity of menu items to ensure that these reflect guests' taste and preferences.

Table 1. The Executive Chef's Responsibilities

Planning	Organizing	Directing	Controlling
Budgeting	Recruiting	Initiating	Auditing
Forecasting	Staffing	Leading	Reporting
Decision making	Hiring	Motivating	Observing
Innovating	Indoctrinating	Supervising	Comparing
Dep. policy making	Training	Communicating	Evaluating
Interpreting	Assigning resources	Providing stimulus	Adjusting
Analyzing			

Source: Guyette, W.C. 1981. The executive chef: Manager or culinarian? The Cornell Hotel and Restaurant Administration Quarterly *22*, 71–76.

2. Supervises and helps train and educate all Chefs and Cooks. Inspects food preparation processes to be sure that these are at proper standards of taste, quality, quantity and appearance.
3. Maintains high standards of sanitation and health-promoting practices in food preparation, storage, personnel, tools and equipment.
4. Requisitions food supplies and kitchen equipment from Steward or Purchasing Agent or directly from salespeople, jobbers or distributors. However, does not receive these for storage as this is done by Receiving Clerk or Assistant Manager.
5. Works closely with Catering Manager or Banquet Manager to create attractive, guest satisfying menus or meals at price levels desired by group's representative.
6. Coordinates with Assistant/Food and Beverage Manager to keep food and some beverage costs within the desired cost/sales ratios. See Table 2. Adjusts menu and portions as needed to maintain desired ratios.

Equipment Used

White hat, coat, apron, Chef's tools and preparation equipment.

Table 2. The Executive Chef's Contribution to Profitability

Material control	Production control	Labor control
Preprocessed foods	Work simplification	Absenteeism
Pilferage	Equipment-intensive recipes	Overtime
Seasonal recipes	Assembly-line techniques	Turnover
Cyclical menus	Preproduction procedures	Grievances
Requisitions	Nonduplication	Promotions
Inventorying	Equipment scheduling	Termination
Spoilage	Standardized recipes	Transfer
Storing	Portion control	Performance
Verification	Yield analysis	Scheduling
Overordering	Leftovers	Sanitation
	Overproduction	Safety
	Underproduction	Training
	Equipment location	Productivity
	Preventive maintenance	
	Production procedures	
	Energy usage	

Source: Same as Table 1.

Working Conditions

Sometimes quite warm to hot. Often provided with a private office near or adjacent to kitchen.

Relation to Other Jobs (See Fig. 1.)

Promotion from: Sous Chef, Chef
Promotion to: Assistant Manager, Assistant/Food and Beverage Manager, General Manager

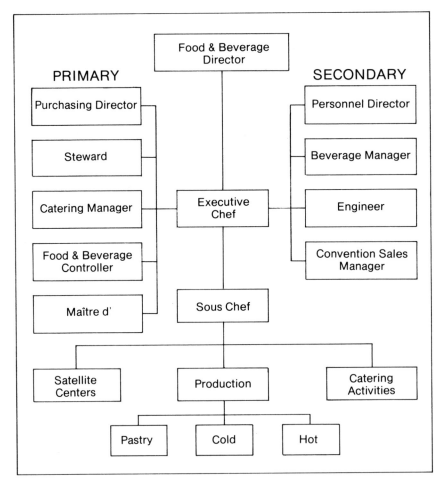

FIG. 1.   The position of the executive chef within the organization.
Courtesy of Guyette, W.C. 1981. The executive chef: Manager or culinarian? The Cornell Hotel and Restaurant Administration Quarterly 22, 71–76.

Job Combination

Could be combined with Sous Chef, Steward, Purchasing Agent, Catering Manager.

Special Qualifications

(1) Requires deep knowledge of all aspects of the culinary arts, including menu making, sales considerations, enticing foods for the geographical location, correct nomenclature for all foods, attractive food descriptions for the menu. (2) Must effectively lead the kitchen staff. (3) Must conduct all functions of kitchen in highest traditions of the art and science of good cookery. (4) Needs to promote efficient production at the determined cost levels. (5) Often has adequate education and successful experience as a Second Cook, First Cook, Baker, Sous Chef, etc., before promotion to Executive Chef.

Supervision

Supervised by: Assistant/Food and Beverage Manager or Director, General Manager
Supervises: All Chefs and Cooks and all other kitchen staff

First Cook

Job Summary

Estimates food consumption, plans menus, and may order foodstuffs; supervises and assists Cooks in preparing, cooking and serving meats, sauces, vegetables, soups and cold foods.

Tasks Performed

1. Plans meals; makes up menus, considering foodstuffs on hand, popularity of dishes, and recent menus; assigns prices to articles on menu.
2. Determines needed foodstuffs, purchases them from salesmen or a market, and checks them for quality and quantity. (The worker cooperates closely with the Manager of the foodservice in the above duties; may act in an advisory capacity only.)
3. Directs Cook, Kitchen Helper, or other kitchen employees in the preparation of vegetables, salads, sandwiches or other foods (except meats) for cooking and serving.
4. Cuts, trims, bones, lards, or otherwise prepares meats and poultry for cooking; makes individual cuts of meat to a specified size or weight, utilizing every possible portion of the carcass.
5. Cooks foods that require skillful preparation, such as roasts, stews, sauces and soups. (Frequently the worker seasons and begins the cooking of such foods and leaves them for an assistant to watch and remove from the fire when cooked.)
6. Tastes all cooked foods; either portions cooked foods or gives instructions as to the size of portions and method of garnishing; usually carves meats.
7. Supervises Cooks (one of whom is usually a Short-Order Cook) and usually a Dishwasher, Kitchen Helper, and Salad or Pantry Worker; employs and discharges workers; trains new employees; keeps time and payroll records.

Desserts and pastries may be prepared by a Pastry Cook, who is supervised by the worker, or they may be purchased from outside. Bread and rolls are usually purchased from outside although they may be prepared by a Pastry Cook, Baker or Cook.

In a large foodservice, the worker might have charge of a supplementary or satellite kitchen, such as a cafeteria kitchen, working under the general supervision of an Executive Chef. If such a situation prevailed, the worker might bear such title as Cafeteria Chef.

Usually there is no Steward employed in a foodservice in which the Chef is a working Chef, such as the Cafeteria Chef described above. The worker would, in such a case, supervise all employees of the Food Preparation Department. In larger establishments, where the cooking is more highly specialized, the worker would devote more time to supervisory duties, and perhaps, to buying foodstuffs. In very large restaurants or in clubs if he/she did no cooking, he/she would be called an Executive Chef.

Equipment Used

Refrigerators, freezers and meat cutting block; meat cutting knives; cleavers and saws; one or more gas or electric cooking ranges; mixing bowls; pots, pans, skillets, spoons, ladles, scales and other standard kitchen equipment; often various mechanical devices for slicing, grinding or mixing foods; sometimes a personal set of carving knives and sharpening hones; white hat, coat and apron; clerical supplies

Material Used

Foodstuffs of all kinds

Working Conditions

Hazards: Superficial burns or scalds from hot stoves, utensils, or foods, also cuts from knives or saws

Relation to Other Jobs

Promotion from: Cook, Short-Order Cook, Dinner Cook, Second Cook, or Roast Cook
Promotion to: Supervising Chef, Executive Chef, Maître d'
Transfer from and to: Sous Chef (in a larger establishment)

Job Breakdown

In larger establishments the duties of this job are divided between specialists such as Steward, Executive Chef, Meat Butcher, and Cooks of various foodstuffs.

Job Combination

The duties of this job may be combined with those of Cook, Short-Order Cook, Baker, Pastry Cook, Breakfast Cook or Dinner Cook.

Special Qualifications

(1) Should possess the ability to cut meat, plan meals and menus that will utilize leftovers, and to cook meats, sauces, and vegetables. (2) Also should have a knowledge of the problems relevant to the management of a kitchen, marketing, composing menus, employing and discharging personnel. (3) May be required to speak, read, and write French or Spanish.

Special Considerations (See footnote 2, p. 154.)

How many Cooks and other employees are supervised? Is worker required to furnish own tools? Is worker responsible for the profit made from the service of food? If so, what ratio of food costs to selling price has been experienced? Does worker compose menus? What types of cooking or frying equipment are operated? Is worker required to plan, prepare and portion food for banquets or other special events? Is worker required to furnish own recipes or use those of the foodservice? Does employer or worker specialize in preparing any special dishes—such as planked steak? Is worker required to bake pastries or breads, or to supervise their baking?

Supervision

Supervised by: Executive Chef, Chef, Sous Chef, Assistant/Food and Beverage Manager
Supervises: Cook Helper, Short-Order Cook, Dishwasher, Salad or Pantry Worker

Fry Cook

Job Summary

Fries meats, fish, fowl, eggs and vegetables in deep or shallow fat.

Tasks Performed

1. Estimates supplies needed from menu; requisitions supplies from storeroom and directs Vegetable Preparer, Vegetable Cook or Fry Cook Apprentice to prepare foods for frying.
2. Fries foods in deep fat or shallow fat; tests heat of vegetable oil or grease in deep-fat fryer with an immersion thermometer and regulates heat accordingly; or sets thermostatic control to regulate heat of grease.
3. Issues fried foods to Waiters: Places food on a warm plate or platter. May season food, garnish platter, or add a gravy or sauce if called for on order.
4. Supervises one or more Fry Cook Apprentices, Vegetable Cooks or Vegetable Preparers, who prepare vegetables for frying and who may assist in frying. French-fried foods should be served as soon as possible after frying and are usually cooked to order. Onions and potatoes are the vegetables most frequently fried.

Equipment Used

Gas or electric ranges; deep-fat fryers; frying pans; skillets; forks, knives, ladles and other kitchen equipment; immersion thermometer

Material Used

Meat, fish, poultry, vegetables, and fruits ready for frying; vegetable oil or grease; seasonings, gravies, sauces and garnishings

Working Conditions

Surroundings: Inside, in extremely hot surroundings, bending over a hot stove or deep-fat fryer. Often heavy smoke from hot grease. At times, must work at high speed, frying two or more foods at once.
Hazards: Burns or scalds from flying grease or from stove or utensils

Relation to Other Jobs

Promotion from: Vegetable Cook, Breakfast Cook, Short-Order Cook, Cook Apprentice, Cook Helper, Vegetable Preparer
Promotion to: Roast Cook, Broiler Cook, Garde-Manger, Dinner Cook, First Cook
Transfer from and to: Breakfast Cook or Broiler Cook

Job Combination

The duties of this job may be combined with those of Vegetable Cook, Vegetable Preparer, Cook Apprentice, Cook Helper, Breakfast Cook, Meat Butcher.

Supervision

Supervised by: Executive Chef, Sous Chef, Assistant/Food and Beverage Manager
Supervises: Cook Helper, Vegetable Preparer

Chef Garde-Manger

Job Summary

Prepares and garnishes cold meat, fish, and poultry dishes, attempting to create appetizing and tasteful dishes out of leftover foods; prepares appetizers, hors d'oeuvres, relishes and salad dressings; may prepare cold sauces, pickles, jellies and stuffings.

Tasks Performed

1. Plans future meals: Notes foods left over from previous meals; confers with individuals in charge of planning menus to decide upon dishes that will utilize as many leftovers as possible; if additional foodstuffs are necessary, requisitions them from storeroom.
2. Carves cold meats: Slices cold roast beef, tongue, corned beef, ham, chicken or other meats; decorates the dish with lettuce, pickles, relishes or other garnishes, and places in refrigerator or on serving table for Waiters.
3. Prepares meat loaves, salads, croquettes, and other dishes that will utilize leftover foods, especially meats, fish and poultry. Chops up, grinds, shreds, slices or dices meat and mixes it with chopped-up onions, celery, potatoes, lettuce, or other vegetables, mixes in mayonnaise or other dressing or seasoning; either molds or fashions mixture into patties or portions of desired size; garnishes each portion or gives it to Cook to be cooked. The above dishes are usually made according to general recipes but these must of necessity be varied according to the foods that are on hand. The ability to prepare tasty dishes of appetizing appearance within such limitations requires considerable experience, ingenuity and artistic ability.
4. May apply hot or cold sauces, made by Second Cook, to above dishes.
5. Prepares salad dressings, such as mayonnaise, French or Russian: Mixes together ingredients according to recipe and seasons them to taste.
6. Prepares appetizers or hors d'oeuvres, such as canapes, or relishes such as olives, celery and pickles. (Ingredients such as caviar, used in canapes, frequently are purchased in prepared form.) The worker spreads these on fancy wafers and thin slices of bread, cuts these into fancy shapes and garnishes them. In many instances relishes are served in more or less elaborately iced dishes.
7. Sometimes prepares cold sauces, pickles, jellies (especially aspic), and stuffings; breads (moistens and covers with bread crumbs) cutlets or other meats.
8. May prepare, or supervise the preparation of, sandwiches, especially those containing cold meats.
9. May supervise one or more Garde-Manger Assistants or Pantry Clerks.

(*Canape*: An appetizer made of a small piece of fresh or toasted bread, spread with fish paste, caviar, or some other delicacy, and usually garnished.)

Equipment Used

Knives, spoons, platters, bowls and other kitchen utensils; work table and refrigerators; sometimes hand or electrically powered meat slicing or grinding machine; white coat, hat and apron

Material Used

Raw and cooked meats and vegetables; seasonings and crushed ice

Working Conditions

Surroundings: Inside in kitchen, frequently a limited space. May be hot from nearby steam cookers, cooking ranges or grills.

Relation to Other Jobs

Promotion from: Garde-Manger Assistant, Meat Butcher, Fry Cook
Promotion to: Second Cook, Sous Chef

Job Combination

The duties of this job may be combined with those of Garde-Manger Assistant, Pantry Worker, Chicken and Fish Butcher, Meat Butcher, Roast Cook, or may be included in those of Dinner Cook.

Special Qualifications

Should possess (1) a knowledge of the various cuts of meat; (2) the ability to improvise new dishes utilizing leftover foods; and (3) the ability to decorate and garnish dishes artistically and to prepare salads, sandwiches and appetizers. (4) Sometimes needs a knowledge of French, Spanish, German and/or Italian. (5) Usually needs an apprenticeship. (6) Must have keen sense of taste to determine when dishes are properly seasoned.

Special Considerations (See footnote 2, p. 154.)

Does worker prepare fancy dishes for banquets or elaborate buffets?

Supervision

Supervised by: Executive Chef, Sous Chef, Assistant/Food and Beverage Manager
Supervises: Cook Helper

Pastry Cook

Job Summary

Mixes batter and prepares and bakes cakes, cookies, pies, compotes, and other confections, pastries, and desserts.

Tasks Performed

Prepares a wide variety of baked products such as pastries, pies, breads, candies and desserts of all kinds. (Where Pie Makers, Dessert Cooks, Bakers or Ice Cream Makers are employed, they make pies, desserts, breads, and ices, leaving cakes, cookies and French pastries to be made and baked by the Pastry Cooks.)

Equipment Used

Mixer; oven; peelers; mixing bowls; knives; rolling pins; work bench; refrigerator; scales; measuring cups and spoons; sifter; gas, electric and microwave ovens; egg beater; spatulas of various sizes and shapes; cream bags and tubes; cake pans; large flat pans for baking cookies and pastries; cookie cutters; air whip. Sometimes proof boxes, a divider, biscuit cutters, pie pans, a pie dough roller, steam kettle, a freezer, molds, and other tools and equipment used by the Baker, Dessert Cook and Pie Maker.

Material Used

Sugar, pastry flour, butter, eggs, shortening, milk, jellies, fruits, flavoring extracts and similar ingredients used to make pastries

Working Conditions

Surroundings: Inside; can be very warm
Hazards: Minor burns from oven or hot pans

Relation to Other Jobs

Promotion from: Pastry Cook Helper, Pie Maker, Dessert Cook
Promotion to: Pastry Chef

Job Combination

The duties of this job may be combined with those of Baker, Dessert Cook, Pie Maker, or Pastry Cook Helper, or they may be included with those of Pastry Chef or Chef.

Special Qualifications

Should possess the ability to prepare and bake pies, cakes, pastries, and desserts of all kinds in quantity. Should know how to execute decorative designs.

Supervision

Supervised by: Executive Chef, Sous Chef, Assistant/Food and Beverage Manager
Supervises: Cook Assistant

Relief Cook

Job Summary

Substitutes for or assists Second Cook, Garde-Manger, Roast Cook, Broiler Cook, Fry Cook, Vegetable Cook or Soup Cook during illness, vacations, or rush periods. This job exists only in large establishments or could be a part-time position.

Tasks Performed

See Tasks Performed for Cooks named above.

Equipment Used

Cooking ranges, grills, kitchen utensils, and equipment used by any of the various Cooks; white hat, coat and apron.

Working Conditions

Surroundings: Inside in usually hot surroundings; exposure to the conditions prevalent at the station of the Cook being relieved
Hazards: Burns from hot stoves, utensils or foods; cuts

Relation to Other Jobs

Promotion from: Any cooking job
Promotion to: Sous Chef, Chef, Second Cook

Special Qualifications

Should possess a first-hand knowledge of all cooking jobs.

Supervision

Supervised by: Executive Chef, Sous Chef, Assistant/Food and Beverage Manager
Supervises: Cook Assistant, Dishwasher, Kitchen Helper

Second Cook

Job Summary

Prepares, cooks, and serves meats and vegetables as directed by Chef or Manager; may bake pastries and hot breads and make cooked desserts; may supervise a Dishwasher or Kitchen Helper. Is typically employed in a small foodservice.

Tasks Performed

1. Fries, boils, broils, or steams vegetables and meats to prepare dishes called for on day's menu; usually cooks simpler dishes, such as fried and boiled foods; tends and removes from fire roasts, stews, sauces, and other more difficult dishes that have been started by the First Cook or Chef.
2. Prepares salads, sandwiches, griddle cakes, fruit juices, and coffee; may bake pastries and breads; and cook desserts.
3. Portions cooked foods and serves them to Waiters upon order.
4. Usually supervises a Dishwasher or Kitchen Helper who prepares vegetables for cooking, cleans utensils and equipment, and performs other miscellaneous duties of a similar nature. (Meats are usually cut and prepared by the Chef or purchased ready prepared.)

(The Second Cook usually cooks all short orders, including such breakfast dishes as eggs and hot cereals, although in some places a separate Short-Order Cook or Breakfast Cook may also be employed.)

Equipment Used

Refrigerator; one or more types of cooking equipment; mixing bowls; pots, pans, skillets, spoons, ladles, scales, and other standard kitchen equipment; sometimes various mechanical devices for cutting, slicing, stirring, grinding, or mixing foods; griddle; and grill

Material Used

Foodstuffs of all kinds

Working Conditions

Surroundings: Inside in usually hot surroundings near cooking ranges and grill; sometimes in a limited space; sometimes rapid work for several hours at a time
Hazards: Superficial burns or scalds from hot surfaces, utensils, or foods

Relation to Other Jobs

Promotion from: Kitchen Helper, Steam-Table Attendant, Breakfast Cook, Cook Assistant
Promotion to: Chef

Job Combination

The duties of this job may be combined with those of Short-Order Cook, Counterman/Counterwoman, Kitchen Helper, or may be included with those of Chef.

Special Qualifications

Ability to prepare, cook, and serve, in quantity, common meats and vegetables using standard recipes.

Special Considerations (See footnote 2, p. 154.)

What are the types and makes of cooking equipment used in the kitchen? What mechanical equipment, such as mixers and slicers, does worker operate? Does worker do all short-order cooking, or is a Short-Order Cook also employed? Is worker required to prepare all vegetables? Meats? Is worker required to clean utensils and equipment? Will worker be the only individual doing cooking? Is worker expected to furnish own recipes or use those of the foodservice? Does worker prepare salads, cooked desserts, sauces, roasts? Does worker bake? Are there any specialties that the worker will be required to cook? Does worker furnish own uniform and tools (knives, steel, etc.)?

Supervision

Supervised by: Executive Chef, Sous Chef, Chef, Assistant/Food and Beverage Manager
Supervises: Cook Assistant, Dishwasher, Kitchen Helper

Short-Order Cook

Job Summary

Cooks to order and serves to Waiters/Waitresses or to guests over counter, steaks, chops, cutlets, eggs and other quickly prepared foods; may also serve roasts, stews, soups, sauces, or vegetables from a steam table; could work in cafeteria, grill, or coffee shop.

Tasks Performed

1. Receives verbal orders from Waiters/Waitresses or customers for chops, steaks, egg dishes, hot cakes, cutlets or other foods that may be quickly prepared.
2. Cooks foods to fill orders.
3. May prepare to order sandwiches, fruit juices, toast, coffee, salads, and other similar dishes.
4. May serve hot roasts, stews, soups, sauces, and vegetables from a steam table, ordering replenishments from main kitchen as necessary.
5. May assist Cooks in main kitchen to prepare and cook food, such as roasts, sauces, soups and vegetables.

(The worker may act as an assistant to the Cook, doing all frying and cooking of breakfasts and helping to prepare and cook roasts, vegetables and other such foods. Occasionally the worker is employed in the pantry or at the serving counter, but only when the pantry or counter is so far removed from the kitchen that short orders cooked in the kitchen would become cold before being served.)

Equipment Used

Small gas stove that may be equipped with a hot plate or grill; refrigerator, griddle, frying pans; gas broiler; deep-fat fryer; knives, forks, spoons; chinaware; glassware; spatulas; steam table; counter; coffee urn; sink; sometimes a cash register; white hat, jacket and apron

Working Conditions

Surroundings: Inside; in front of a hot stove and grill; frequently at high speed, cooking several orders at once
Hazards: Superficial burns from hot stove or from flying grease

Relation to Other Jobs

Promotion from: Counterman/Counterwoman, Kitchen Helper, Pantry Worker, Pot Washer
Promotion to: Cook, Fry Cook, Chef, Meat Cook, Roast Cook, Assistant to any Cook, Broiler Cook, Garde-Manger Assistant
Transfer from and to: Breakfast Cook, or Cook

Job Combination

The duties of this job may be combined with those of Breakfast Cook, Counterman/Counterwoman, Vegetable Cook, Vegetable Preparer, Coffee Preparer, Pantry Worker, Cook, Fry Cook, Dinner Cook, Broiler Cook, Kitchen Helper, or they may be included with those of Chef.

Special Qualifications

(1) Ability to cook a number of separate orders at one time without confusion, and (2) ability to cook all kinds of short orders rapidly.

Supervision

Supervised by: Executive Chef, Sous Chef, Chef, Assistant/Food and Beverage Manager
Supervises: Cook Assistant, Dishwasher, Kitchen Helper

Pantry Worker or Salad Maker

Job Summary

Prepares salads, fruit or vegetable juice, cocktails, canapes, and other cold dishes usually before lunch or dinner time, and serves them to Waiters/Waitresses during meals; makes sandwiches on short order or in quantities; prepares tea and coffee (hot or iced) and other beverages; slices cold meats and cheeses and portions them to Waiters/Waitresses and supplies them with desserts and side dishes such as bread and butter; may serve hot food portions to Waiters/Waitresses from a steam table.

Tasks Performed

1. Prepares salads and cocktails: Washes fruit and vegetables, peels them if necessary, and chops, cuts or dices them; slices cold meats and prepares seafood by removing shells or bones and cutting up into pieces of convenient size; may obtain salad ingredients from cans; places pieces of lettuce on serving plates and the ingredients on the lettuce, arranging them in an attractive manner; mixes dressings, sauces and garnishes and adds them to the salad.
2. Makes sandwiches.
3. Supplies Waiters/Waitresses during meals: Gives them salads, cocktails, canapes, butter, bread and rolls, desserts and other cold food dishes; makes and pours coffee, tea and other beverages (hot or iced) into cups or glasses; may portion hot foods from a steam table; may dispense dry cereals, boiled eggs, waffles, pancakes, condiments and other food items easily prepared.
4. Cleans equipment: Places waste food in garbage cans, cleans counters and work area with a damp cloth, and scours, cleans and polishes fixtures and equipment.
5. May requisition food supplies.

Equipment Used

Assorted knives; cubing, shredding, and grating devices; refrigerators; electric bread toasters; coffee urn; serving plates; steam table

Material Used

Salad, cocktail, canape, and sandwich ingredients

Working Conditions

Surroundings: Inside, may be hot from steam table and other hot equipment
Hazards: Possibility of cuts from salad chopping knives and burns from hot equipment

Relation to Other Jobs

Promotion from: Dishwasher, Glass Washer, Silver Washer, Vegetable Preparer, Kitchen Helper
Promotion to: Pantry Supervisor, Short-Order Cook, Food Checker (Dining Room), Pastry Cook Assistant, Cashier, Hostess, Waiter or Waitress (Informal), Garde-Manger Assistant, Pie Maker, Counter Supervisor, Steward(ess)
Transfer from and to: Counterman/Counterwoman, Dessert Cook, Sandwich Preparer, Coffee Preparer

Job Breakdown

The duties of this job may be divided between a Salad Maker, Steam-Table Attendant, Pantry Supervisor, Sandwich Preparer, Dessert Cook, Breakfast Cook and Coffee Preparer.

Job Combination

The duties of this job may be combined with those of Garde-Manger Assistant, Pastry Cook Helper, Counterman/Counterwoman, Coffee Preparer.

Supervision

Supervised by: Pantry Supervisor, Short-Order Cook, Chef, Cooks

Vegetable Preparer or Cook Assistant

Job Summary

Prepares vegetables for cooking by chopping, cutting, dicing, peeling, grinding, or mashing them; operates peeling and other mechanical equipment; services and cleans equipment. May utilize frozen vegetables.

Tasks Performed

1. Receives instructions from Vegetable Cook and other Cooks as to kind and amount of different vegetables to be prepared and the manner in which they are to be prepared.
2. Procures vegetables from storeroom or refrigerator, and inspects them for freshness, selecting those most appropriate in size, shape and color or quality for the purposes for which they are to be used.
3. Peels tuber vegetables, such as potatoes, turnips, beets and carrots with a mechanical peeler; trims each vegetable with a paring knife to remove eyes and washes vegetables. Operates additional machines such as a "dicer," which cubes vegetables, a French fry cutter, which cuts "hard" vegetables into rectangular shapes, and a masher, which mashes or rices vegetables; gives vegetables to Cooks.
4. Cleans and prepares green vegetables such as spinach, cabbage, artichokes, peas, and beans, rinses them several times to separate leaves and to wash off dirt and sand; uses a paring knife to cut away inedible or bruised portions; places vegetables on Cooks' table.
5. Opens canned goods placing vegetables in appropriate containers, and putting them on table.
6. May remove skins from tomatoes, beets, and turnips by immersing them momentarily in boiling water to loosen the skins and peeling them off with paring knife.
7. Cleans equipment and scrubs table and utensils; collects inedible pieces of vegetables and puts them in the garbage pail or chute; may assist Pot Washer during slack periods.
8. May, upon direction by any Cook, prepare leftover meats for soups and stews; places meat upon block and trims off undesirable parts with a cleaver or knife.

Relation to Other Jobs

Transfer from and to: Other jobs in the kitchen and dining room not requiring experience such as Kitchen Helper, Butcher Helper or Bus Boy or Girl

Job Combination

The duties of this job may be included in those of Short-Order Cook, Vegetable Cook, Cook Apprentice, and may be combined with those of Pot Washer, Kitchen Helper and Dishwasher.

Special Qualifications

This is usually a beginning job for which experience is not required.

Supervision

Supervised by: Chefs, Cooks

KITCHEN OPERATION

Dishwasher/Sanitation Assistant

Job Summary

Removes leftover food from dishes into disposal equipment; washes and rinses dishes in dish machine; removes and sorts dishes into appropriate groups; delivers dishes to designated areas for reuse. May also wash silverware, glassware, trays, and pots−pans.

Tasks Performed

1. Receives soiled dishes from Waitresses, Waiters, Bus Boys/Girls.
2. Handles dishes in orderly fashion, taking care to protect dishes from rough handling to minimize damage to dishes.
3. Scrapes or otherwise removes any leftover from dishes and places dishes in appropriate racks in preparation to insertion in dish machine.
4. Checks condition of machine as to water temperature (should be at 180°F), supply level of detergent and working condition of machine. (There are cold-water chemical sanitizing dish machines available, also.)
5. Places dish racks in machine, using proper procedures designated for machine by manufacturer and by health department.
6. Upon completion of washing cycle, removes racks; inspects dishes for cleanliness; removes dishes from racks; sorts dishes; and carries dishes to appropriate storage areas.
7. Maintains proper level of cleanliness of dish machine area; immediately picking up from floor any garbage or other hazardous material which might cause anyone walking near dish machine to slip and fall; wipes and cleans working areas and tables; may do other cleaning and maintenance chores in kitchen as designated by the Kitchen Steward.

Equipment Used

Dish machine and dish racks; dish towels and cloths; cleaning hose and scrapers; floor cleaning equipment for quick pickups; aprons and caps furnished by employer

Materials Used

Detergent and other cleaning and chemical agents such as spot dispersal agents and sanitizers

Working Conditions

Standing most of the time; constantly working with hot water; often warm to hot conditions with steam and vapors present; dishes hot from the machine and often gloves needed protect hands.

Possible hazards: Burns or cuts

Relation to Other Jobs

Promotion to: Pantry Worker, Silver Washer, Coffee Preparer, Waiter/Waitress (Informal), Steward

Job Combination

Duties of this job are frequently combined with those of Pot Washer or Silver Washer.

Special Qualifications

This is a beginning job and no previous experience is necessary. However, the applicant selected should have good sanitary standards and want to keep things clean and neat. Often a handicapped person or with somewhat low intelligence will do an outstanding job in this position.

Supervision

Supervised by: Kitchen Steward, Cooks

Glass Washer

Job Summary

Washes and rinses glassware in an automatic glass washing machine; dries and sorts clean glassware. May work in bar or service bars for special parties or functions.

Tasks Performed

1. Prepares glassware for washing: Empties liquids left in glasses and scrapes glassware such as pitchers, plates and dishes, as clean as possible; separates glasses according to size; places glassware in sectioned glass racks.
2. Washes glassware in machine: Opens door of glass washing machine; slides loaded glass rack into machine, lowering doors into position; switches on motor and throws small lever to admit soap solution to tank, allowing solution to run from two to three minutes; turns off soap solution and, by pulling lever in opposite direction, admits rinse water allowing it to run from 2 to 3 minutes; stops rinse water; removes glassware compartment.
3. Sorts individual pieces according to type.
4. Cleans and maintains machine and other equipment at frequent intervals.

Materials Used

Detergents, spot dispersal agent, scouring powder, metal polish, drying cloths

Working Conditions

Standing most of the time; occasionally getting wet when removing glassware from machine; atmosphere hot and humid
Possible hazard: Broken glass

Relation to Other Jobs

Promotion to: Pantry Worker, Coffee Preparer, Waiter/Waitress, Steward
Transfer from and to: Dishwasher, Pot Washer, Kitchen Helper

Job Combination

The duties of this job are frequently combined with those of Dishwasher, Pot Washer, Silver Washer.

Special Qualifications

A beginning job requiring no experience.

Supervision

Supervised by: Kitchen Steward

Kitchen Helper

Job Summary

Cleans kitchen; helps kitchen employees and Cooks; prepares raw foods for cooking.

Tasks Performed

1. Scrubs, scrapes, and scours work tables, meat blocks, and refrigerators; cleans and sweeps floors.
2. Carries dirty cooking utensils to Pot Washer and returns cleaned utensils to Cook.
3. Performs miscellaneous jobs such as carrying garbage and carrying supplies.
4. May strain soups and sauces; make toast and beverages; wash and clean meats and vegetables; peel, pare, or string vegetables; watch and stir foods that are cooking; and otherwise relieve Cook of simple routine duties while gaining familiarity with kitchen procedure.
5. Works under the close supervision of a Chef, Cook or Dinner Cook.

Equipment Used

Pail; mop; broom; cleaning and polishing brushes and cloths; scraper; sink; paring knives; may use stoves, pots, pans, skillets and other Cooks' equipment

Material Used

Water; soap powder and other cleaning and scouring agents; utensils and equipment to be cleansed

Working Conditions

Surroundings: Working in kitchen usually hot and humid from cooking equipment and scrubbing and scouring work benches and floors
Hazards: Superficial burns from hot surfaces or utensils

Relation to Other Jobs

Promotion from: Dishwasher
Promotion to: Cook Apprentice, Cook Assistant, Cook, Short-Order Cook, Chicken and Fish Butcher, Vegetable Cook, Storeroom Clerk, Pantry Worker, Coffee Preparer, Waiter/ Waitress
Transfer from and to: Vegetable Preparer, Kitchen Runner, Glass Washer

Job Breakdown

In large establishments the duties of this job may be divided between various specialized Cook Assistants or Apprentices.

Job Combination

The duties of this job may be combined with those of Vegetable Preparer, Dishwasher, Kitchen Runner, Bus Boy/Girl, Coffee Preparer, Steam-Table Attendant, or they may be included with the duties of Short-Order Cook, Cook, Cleaner or Porter.

Special Qualifications

This is usually a beginning job for which experience is not required.

Supervision

Supervised by: Chefs, Cooks, Kitchen Steward

Kitchen Steward or Steward

Job Summary

Closely supervises the kitchen, pantry, and storeroom employees not actively engaged in cooking, such as Dishwashers, Pantry Workers and Storeroom Helpers to ensure cleanliness, economy, and honesty; assists subordinates when necessary. May also order supplies and equipment.

Tasks Performed

1. Inspects kitchen, pantries, storerooms and employees; dining rooms to see that premises and equipment are clean and in order and that sufficient food and other supplies are on hand to ensure efficient service; requisitions additional supplies when necessary.
2. Supervises and assigns work to Dishwashing Crew, Pantry and Storeroom Workers, and other employees (except Chefs and Cooks) engaged in food preparation; keeps time and production records for these workers; may employ and discharge workers; assists subordinates when necessary; instructs new employees.

3. Takes inventories of china, silverware, and glassware, attempting to guard against theft and breakage; reports shortages and requisitions replacements of equipment from Purchasing Agent, or performs this requisition function.
4. Assists Food Checkers to make sure that food is properly garnished and arranged on dishes, and that dishes are properly arranged on trays.
5. Requisitions supplies such as brushes, mops and soap.
6. May arrange for table linen, china, silverware, glassware, for the preparation of salads, coffee, fruit juices—pantry service—for banquets or other special occasions.

Relation to Other Jobs

Promotion from: Storeroom Clerk, Food Checker (Dining Room), Coffee Preparer, Glass Washer, Silver Washer, Dishwasher, Pantry Worker
Promotion to: Purchasing Agent, Banquet Steward

Job Combination

The duties of this job may be combined with those of Storeroom Clerk or Food Checker.

Special Qualifications

(1) Should possess high standards of cleanliness and be quick to recognize unsanitary or unsafe conditions and act immediately to correct such situations; (2) should understand operations of dish machine and silver cleaning machine; (3) must have a general knowledge of cooking and garnishing and the care of perishable foods and a first-hand knowledge of all noncooking jobs in kitchen, storerooms and pantry; and (4) be able to efficiently order supplies.

Supervision

Supervised by: Executive Chef, Assistant/Food and Beverage Manager
Supervises: Kitchen Helper, Dishwasher, Glass Washer, Tray Washer

Tray Washer

Job Summary

Washes dining room trays and performs other miscellaneous duties in and about kitchen.

Tasks Performed

1. Separates trays received from dining room and other food areas into those to be washed and those to be wiped only.
2. Washes trays in hot, soapy water; wipes washed trays with a dish towel; wipes other trays with a damp cloth and then with a dry towel.
3. Stacks all trays.
4. May make silverware sets by selecting a knife, fork and spoon and wrapping them in a cloth or paper napkin.
5. Assists in sweeping, mopping, and window washing.

Working Conditions

Hazards: Scalds from hot water

Relation to Other Jobs

Transfer from and to: Pot Washer, Dishwasher

Special Qualifications

This is usually a beginning job for which experience is not required.

Supervision

Supervised by: Kitchen Steward, Cooks

OFFICE AND BUILDING

Bookkeeper

Job Summary

Keeps a complete and systematic set of all foodservice transactions. Makes individual entries pertaining to charges, receipts and disbursements. From the total of charges and receipts, keeps a general ledger which represents the current amount of the foodservice's business.

Tasks Performed

1. Verifies all cash in the establishment's cash system.
2. Reviews all cash pay outs and posts to ledger in mechanical or by electronic means.
3. Checks charge documents, vouchers, and cash sheets with transcripts and accounts to see that no errors occur in posting.
4. Audits all bills or invoices and pays with voucher checks.
5. Enters checks for bills paid with amounts in check journal.
6. Enters amounts of bills paid in the general ledger under their classified headings so that management can determine how much has been spent for different items.
7. Petty cash items may be posted in this ledger to the same accounts.

Type of Bookkeeping System

Uniform System of Accounts manuals
Reports prepared: Tax returns, income reports, sales reports, social security reports, balance sheets, profit and loss reports, bank reconciliations, other reports required by state or federal government
Other records kept: Credit accounts, employees time records

Office Machines

Adding machine, calculating machine, computer, printer, typewriter

Related Work

Prepare correspondence; prepare payroll; file papers; prepare, type and mail statements

Relation to Other Jobs

This job may be added to the usual duties of Office Manager, Accountant, or Controller.

Supervision

Supervised by: Office Manager, General Manager
Supervises: Clerks, Secretaries

Purchasing Director

Job Summary

Purchases foodstuffs, kitchen supplies and equipment requisitioned by the Steward, or Executive Chef at the best possible market price; supervises storage of foodstuffs.

Tasks Performed

1. Receives written requisitions from Executive Chef or Steward for needed foodstuffs and supplies. May also order for Bartender.
2. Purchases foodstuffs and supplies, typical of which are kitchen utensils, silverware, glassware, china, cleaning supplies and equipment. Either goes to public markets or interviews salesmen who call, or orders by telephone or letter from a jobber, market or retailer; assumes complete responsibility for the quality and price of articles purchased.
3. Inspects incoming supplies and approves for payment the invoices accompanying articles purchased; maintains accounts such as records of the amount spent by each department of the kitchen or bar.
4. Supervises Storeroom Clerks: Sees that supplies are stored properly and in designated places; supervises the taking of inventories; assigns work.
5. Cooperates closely with Steward, Executive Chef, Maître d', and Chef; determines whether too much is being spent for supplies or too little charged for meals, adjusting purchases accordingly or consulting the individual who prices menus; receives notification of food supplies needed for banquets or other special occasions and purchases these supplies.
6. Reads daily market quotations and trade journals to keep informed of market conditions.

(This job exists only in very large foodservices. In smaller ones, foodstuffs are purchased by the Steward, Chef or Executive Chef and other commodities are purchased by the separate department heads. In some instances, the Purchasing Agent also purchases liquors, linens, and uniforms. However, such supplies are usually purchased by the separate department heads.)

Relation to Other Jobs

Promotion from: Storeroom Clerk, Steward
Promotion to: Maître d', Accountant

Job Combination

The duties of this job may be combined with those of Steward or Storeroom Clerk, or included with those of Steward, Executive Chef, Manager, Maître d', or Accountant.

Special Qualifications

Must have (1) knowledge of simple bookkeeping; (2) practical knowledge of foodstuffs and other commodities used; (3) knowledge of the care of perishable foodstuffs; (4) knowledge of current market conditions; (5) knowledge of principles of management.

Special Considerations (See footnote 2, p. 154.)

Does worker purchase supplies other than foodstuffs and kitchen supplies? What employees will be supervised?

Supervision

Supervised by: Office Manager, General Manager
Supervises: Storeroom Clerks, Office Clerks, Secretaries

Receiving Clerk

Job Summary

Receives and inspects incoming foodstuffs and staples to ensure satisfactory delivery; promptly stores goods in proper temperature-controlled areas to prevent losses and issues them in accordance with requisitions; keeps a running inventory and reports shortages to Steward or Purchasing Agent.

Tasks Performed

1. Receives and checks supplies into the storeroom as delivered: Obtains supplies from delivery truck; opens samples of packaged goods to inspect condition of contents; checks delivery order against invoices, noting sizes and quantity and quality of all meats, poultry, vegetables and other merchandise before accepting delivery. Makes notes of shortages or order changes.
2. Stores stock in storeroom of proper temperature; arranges stock on shelves so that oldest supply is utilized first. Keeps storage areas neat and orderly.
3. Receives requisition for supplies, and issues goods in accordance with requisition; may personally deliver to the proper department.
4. Keeps running inventory to prevent shortages, and makes daily report, or requisitions to Purchasing Agent or Steward.
5. Sweeps and cleans storage areas to maintain sanitary conditions.

Equipment Used

Scales; refrigerators; shelves; clipboards; files; measuring utensils

Relation to Other Jobs

Promotion from: Cellarman, Bus Boy/Girl, Kitchen Helper
Promotion to: Steward, Bookkeeper, Purchasing Agent

Job Combination

The duties of this worker may be combined with those of Cellarman, or may be included in those of Purchasing Agent or Steward.

Supervision

Supervised by: Kitchen Steward, Purchasing Agent, Assistant/Food and Beverage Manager

Engineer

Job Summary

Does general repair and maintenance work. May operate heating system, air conditioning and ventilation systems.

Tasks Performed

1. Maintains and makes general repairs to the plumbing fixtures, furniture, woodwork, electrical system and appliances, elevators, ventilation system, and building structure.
2. Paints walls; builds shelves; repairs woodwork and furniture.
3. Installs new electric outlets; repairs electrical appliances.
4. Replaces or repairs leaking pipes and faucets; performs other similar duties usually requiring experience as an all-around Carpenter, Painter, Plumber, and Electrician.
5. May operate and maintain the heating and air conditioning equipment.

(The number of duties performed by one individual usually depends upon the size of the establishment; the duties being more varied in small establishments.)

Equipment Used

Wrenches, saws, planes, pliers, hammers, screw drivers, oil cans, shovel, paint brushes, wiping cloths and other tools depending on the type of work to be done

Material Used

Oil, grease, wire, paint, spigot washers, and other materials needed to accomplish the particular work on hand

Job Breakdown

This job includes the work done in larger establishments by Carpenter, Plumber, Janitor, Painter, Cabinet Maker, Electrician, Fireman.

Special Qualifications

(1) Should be an all-around carpenter, painter, plumber, and electrician. (2) Should be of resourceful, ingenious nature. (3) Also, must be cost conscious to keep energy costs and maintenance expenses at moderate levels.

Supervision

Supervised by: General Manager, Assistant Manager
Supervises: Maintenance Helper

Appendix B

Selected Trade Journals and Book Publishers

FOODSERVICE TRADE JOURNALS

Beverage Industry. 777 Third Avenue New York, NY 10017

Canadian Hotel and Restaurant. Mclean-Hunter Publishing Co., Ltd., 481 University Avenue, Toronto, Ontario M5W 1A7, Canada

Catering Industry Employee. Hotel and Restaurant Employees and Bartenders International Union, 120 East Fourth Street, Cincinnati, OH 45202

Club Management. Commerce Publishing Co., 408 Olive Street, St. Louis, MO 63102

The Cornell Hotel and Restaurant Administration Quarterly. School of Hotel Administration, 327 Statler Hall, Cornell Univ., Ithaca, NY 14853

Lodging and Food Service News. Hotel Service, 131 Clarendon Street, Boston, MA 02116

NRA News. National Restaurant Association, 311 First Street, N.W., Washington, DC 20001

NACUFS Newsletter Digest. National Association of College and Univ. Food Services, c/o Susan Dunlap, Univ. Dining Service, Valparaiso Univ., Valparaiso, IN 46383

Nation's Restaurant News. Lebhar-Friedman, 425 Park Avenue, New York, NY 10022

Restaurant Business. 633 Third Avenue, New York, NY 10017

Restaurant Hospitality. 1111 Chester Avenue, Cleveland, OH 44114

Restaurants and Institutions. Cahners Publishing Co., 5 South Wabash Avenue, Chicago, IL 60603

Security Management. 2000 K Street, N.W., Suite 651, Washington, DC 20006

PERSONNEL AND MANAGEMENT TRADE JOURNALS

Advanced Management. Society for the Advancement of Management, 74 Fifth Avenue, New
     York, NY 10011
Human Relations. Plenum Press, 227 West 17th Street, New York, NY 10011
Journal of Applied Psychology. 1200 17th. St., N.W., Washington, DC 20036
Journal of the American Society of Training Directors. Official publication of the American
     Society of Training Directors, 2020 University Avenue, Madison, WI 53706
Management Review. American Management Association, Box 319, Saranac Lake, NY 12983
Personnel. American Management Association, Box 319, Saranac Lake, NY 12983
Personnel Journal. Box 1520, Santa Monica, CA 90404
Personnel Management Abstracts. Bureau of Industrial Relations, Univ. of Michigan, Ann
     Arbor, MI 48104
Personnel Psychology. P.O. Box 6965, College Station, Durham, NC 27708
Studies in Personnel Policy. National Industrial Conference Board, 247 Park Avenue, New
     York, NY 10017
Supervisory Management. American Management Association, Box 319, Saranac Lake, NY
     12983
Training. Lakewood Publications, 731 Hennepin Avenue, Minneapolis, MN 55403

ADDRESSES OF BOOK PUBLISHERS CITED

Addison-Wesley Publishing Co., One Jacob Way, Reading, MA 01867
Alfred A. Knopf, 201 E. 50th Street, New York, NY 10022
Amacom, American Management Association, 135 West 50th Street, New York, NY 10022
AVI Publishing Co., Inc., 250 Post Road, P.O. Box 831, Westport, CT 06881
CBI Publishing Co., 51 Sleeper St., Boston, MA 02210
Club Managers Association of America, 7615 Winterberry Place, Bethesda, MD 20817
Culinary Institute of America, Hyde Park, NY 12538
D.C. Heath and Co., 125 Spring Street, Lexington, MA 02173
Educational Institute, American Hotel and Motel Association, 310 Stephen Nisbet Bldg.,
     Michigan State Univ., East Lansing, MI 48824
ITT Educational Publishing, 4300 W. 62nd Street, Indianapolis, IN 46278
Lebhar-Friedman Books, 425 Park Avenue, New York, NY 10022
McCutchan Publishing Corp., P.O. Box 77A, Berkeley, CA 94701
Michigan State University Press, East Lansing, MI 48824
National Restaurant Association, 311 First Street, N.W., Washington, DC 20001
Prentice-Hall, Rte. 9W., Englewood Cliffs, NJ 07632
School of Hotel Administration, Cornell Univ., Ithaca, NY 14853
Simon and Schuster, 1230 Avenue of the Americas, New York, NY 10020
South-Western Publishing Co., 5101 Madison Rd., Cincinnati, OH 45227
Survey Research Center, Univ. of Michigan, Ann Arbor, MI 48103
West Publishing Co., 50 W. Kellogg Boulevard, P.O. Box 3526, St. Paul, MN 55165

Index

A

Absenteeism, 21
Affirmative action programs
  80% rule, 70
  employee selection, 70
  handicapped workers, 70-71
  interviewing applicants, 69-70
  laws, 124-125
  tests, 76
Alternative work provisions, 57-61
Appraisal interviews, 97
Apprentice training, 88-89
Armed robbery and burglary, 143-144
Attitudes, 61-62, 80-81, 91
Authority and delegation of, 5

B

Bar operation
  job descriptions (selected), 148-151
  thefts from, 141-142
Being understood, 37-39
Bonuses, 109-110
Book publishers addresses, 190

C

Communication skills, 37-39
  being understood, 37-39
  developing skills, 37-48
  listening, 39-42
  meetings, 11, 43-44
  organization charts, 45-46
  policy manuals, 46-48
  procedural manuals, 48
Compressed work week, 57, 58
Customer count, 53

D

Dialogue training, 84-87

E

Educational upgrading, 95-96
Employee selection, 64-77
  affirmative action, 69-71
  checking references, 136-138
  finding employees, 64-66
  honest employees, 135
  interviewing techniques, 68-70
  personal interviews, 66-70

steps in selecting and hiring, 67
recruiting enticements, 65-66
Employees
abilities, 19
absenteeism, 21
attitudes, 61-62, 80-81, 91
communication with, 37-48
conflicts and compromises, 20-21
evaluation, 96-99
finding, 64-66
firing, 34-35
handicapped, 70
health and nutrition, 61
individual qualities of, 16-20
insurance, 125-126
motivation of, 102-122
needs of, 16-17
placement of, 75-76
quits, 34-36
recognition of, 26-27
rules and regulations, 142-143
satisfactions, 19-20
selecting, 64-77
smoking, 28-29
social intercourse of, 28
stress, 29-31
tardiness, 21
tests, 76-77
thefts by, 138-141
titles, 27
training, 78-100
underused, 62
values of, 17-19
wants from work, 22-24
Enjoying work, 21-22
Evaluating employees, 96-99

F
Finding employees, 64-66
Firing people and quits, 34-35
Flextime, 57, 58
Foodservice trade journals, 189
Forecasting, 54-55
Fringe benefits, 118-120

G
Goal setting
employees, 96-97
handicapped workers, 70

incentives and, 102-104
management, 13

H
Human relations, 16-36

I
Incentives for motivation, 102-109
Insurance for employees, 125-126
Interviewing job applicants, 66-71

J
Japanese theory Z, 10-11
Job analysis helps in hiring, 71
Job descriptions, 71-72
bar and beverage, 148-151
dining room service, 151-163
food preparation, 164-180
kitchen operation, 180-185
office and building, 165-188
selected, 147-188
when to use, 72
Job enrichment programs, 29
Job evaluation for pay equity, 73-74
Job instruction training, 82-84
Job qualities for good work environment, 75
Job satisfaction, 50-51
Job sharing, 57-61
Job specification, 72-73

L
Labor reports, 56
Laws affecting employees, 123-124
Leadership, 1-14
qualities of, 1-2
patterns of, 2-3
styles, 7-11
Learning categories for training, 80-81
Legality of employment records, 124
Legal problems
affirmative action, 124-125
employee's laws, 123-124
employment records, 124
Listening, 39-42
Love, 24

M
Management
art of, 3

bottoms up, 6–7
improvement steps, 50
incentives, 108
participative, 8
philosophy, 104–105
science of, 3
systems approach, 12–14
task-oriented, 9
theory X, 9
theory Y, 8
theory Z, 10
updating knowledge, 14
Managers
assistant, 6, 127
bonuses, 108–110
department heads as, 6
general, 6
incentives for, 108
insurance for, 125
key to security, 127–128
self-discipline of, 6
supervisors as, 6
team approach for, 7, 46
who steal, 127
Managing others, 3, 12–14, 99–100, 104–105
McDonald's Corporation, 58
McGregor's theory X, Y, 8–9
Meetings, 11, 43–44
Motivating employees, 102–122
bonuses, 109–110
incentive programs, 102–109
nonmonetary incentives, 107–108
promotion, 121
retirement, 121–122
Scanlon Plan, 110–114
suggestion system, 109

N
New employee orientation, 46–48

O
On-the-job training, 89
Organization
benefits of good, 44
charts, 44–46, 168
how to achieve good, 44–45

P
Part-time employment, 57, 58
Payroll productivity, 49–51

People person (being one), 4–5
Personnel and management trade
    journals, 190
Placement, 75–76
Policy and procedural manuals, 46–48
Productivity, increasing, 49–62
alternative work provisions, 57–61
definitions, 50
forecasting, 54–55
implementing, 51
improving job, 51
payroll, 49–51
reports, 56–57
setting standards for, 52–54
staff planning and scheduling, 52, 55–56
underused people, 62

Q
Quality of work life, improving, 24–26

R
Recognition of workers, 26–27
Responsibility, 5

S
Salaries, see Wages and salaries
Scanlon incentive plan, 110–114
benefits, 111
disadvantages, 112
example of, 112–114
Selecting employees, 64–76
Scheduling workers, 52–56, 58
Security measures, 126–145
Selecting and hiring job applicants, 66–71
Staffing, 52–61
differentiated, 57–58
planning and scheduling, 52–56
scale of, 55
weekly work schedules, 55
Staff planning and scheduling, 52–56
Stealing methods, 138–142
Stress, 29–31
Supervising staff, 78–100
Supervisors, 1, 4, 5, 6, 11, 20, 23, 30, 34, 36
    40, 44, 72, 81, 89, 99, 100
Systems approach to management, 12–14

T
Tardiness, 21
Tests, 76–77

affirmative action implications, 76
success predictors, 66, 69, 76−77
used in selection, 67
validity, 76
Thank you, 31
Theft prevention and security, 126−145
  armed robbery and burglary, 143−144
  magnitude of problem, 126
  management concern, 127−128
  methods of stealing, 138−142
  selecting honest employees, 135−138
  suggested policies, 128−135, 141−143
  who steals?, 127
Titles, 27
Trade journals and book publishers, 189−190
Training, 78−96
  apprentice, 88
  attitude (affective), 91−92
  check list, 90−95
  conference, 87
  continuity, 89
  definition, 79−80
  determining needs, 79
  dialogue, 84−87
  evaluation, 90
  group instruction, 87−88
  information (cognitive), 91

job instruction, 82−84, 89, 90−95
learning categories, 80−81
manipulative (psycho motor), 91
methods, 82−89
programs, 82−89
role playing, 87
trainers, 81−82
why train?, 78−79

U

Unions, 31−34, 56
Updating knowledge, 14

V

Voluntary, sabbatical, personal leave, 57

W

Wages and salaries, 114−118
  a compensation plan, 116−118
  equitable, 72, 73, 74, 115−117
  fringe benefits, 118−120
  review, 114−116
  secrecy, 115
Wants of employees, 22−24
Work schedules, 54−56
Work sharing, 57, 58−61